Dressing the Story

With Alicia Silverstone working on the theatrical production of
David Mamet's *Boston Marriage* (2005).

To be a costume designer is to live in long days that spill into nights,
in weekends that disappear,
in moments missed, and dreams pursued.
I was warned.

What I could not have known was how much I would depend on love to sustain it.

To my husband, Billy McGuire—my steady ground—whose patience, grace and deep devotion to our children made this life possible.

To Gavin, gifted in many ways, who came to work beside me and deepened our bond in ways I never expected.

To Lily, who lives globally and creatively, weaving her businesses into a life of adventure.

We did not simply endure this life—we thrived.
This book is for you, with all my love.

For Jim Stark—without whom this book could not exist. Sixty years of friendship, deeply held and dearly loved.

ISBN 979-8-89976-079-2

Contents

Foreword by David Mamet

Deb's book brings back the "you had to be there" of show business memories.

In this magnificent dog's dinner of a racket, one not only "had to be there" but, be there as part of the proceedings, else one (a visitor) could have no idea of what was going on.

On a movie set, the producers are always ignorant fools and/or thieves, the hair and makeup trailer is the source of various information and slanders, the first assistant director, if any good, is coming down with ulcers, and the costume department is, comparatively, an oasis, if not of reason, then of intermittent reasonability.

Yes, they have to deal with the anxiety (human and professional), narcissism (likewise), and lies (no actor ever reported his actual weight—all appear aghast at the incomprehensibly constrictive costumes). But the relationship between designer and director is straightforward, consisting of appreciation (on the canny director's part), his sympathy for the designer's fortitude in dealing with the actors, and her character in (generally) not sharing her trauma with the director.

I loved working with Deb. She and her folks got the show into the frocks and the frocks onto the players. God bless her.

A classic moment from *Friends*: Joey puts on all of Chandler's clothes
as revenge for Chandler hiding his underwear.

Introduction

A personal note on costume design, collaboration, and why this book exists.

Film is a visual language, and costume design is one of its most potent dialects. Costumes are not mere clothing but carefully considered elements of storytelling, communicating who a character is before they ever speak a line. They reveal personality, status, transformation, and emotion, often subliminally, but always powerfully. In a career spanning over four decades, I have had the privilege of dressing stories for the screen, collaborating with directors, actors, and crews to bring characters to life through fabric, texture, and silhouette.

This book is a conversation I had with producer Jim Stark about the art and craft of costume design for film and TV. It includes interview material from two members of my team. Joe Mastrolia is my longtime supervisor in the costume departments of nearly all the feature films I have worked on. Joe is a second-generation costumer (his father worked at Warner Bros. in the '70s and '80s) who joined the costume designers' union in 1990, worked his way up to supervisor, and has been a costumer on more than sixty productions. My son, Gavin McGuire, grew up on the sets of the productions I costume designed. He began working on films as a production assistant, joined the costume designers' union in 2010, and has worked on more than 25 films and series as a set costumer and then as the key costumer on set.

Dressing the Story is a reflection on the lessons learned, the challenges met, and the joys found in the process of designing for some of the most iconic productions of our time. It is also an exploration of how costumes become part of the visual architecture of a film, working in concert with cinematography, production design, and direction to shape the viewer's experience.

Whether you are a designer, a filmmaker, or simply someone who loves film, these conversations aim to illuminate the often invisible artistry that costume design brings to the screen.

Debra McGuire

That's me on the left, in *Anchorman*, with Paul Rudd,
uttering the classic line, "Smells like Bigfoot's dick."

Becoming a Designer
Early influences, art school, and finding my voice in design

Did you always know you would be a costume designer?

I didn't begin my creative journey with the intention of becoming a costume designer. My early years were spent in the world of fine art, studying painting and printmaking at the California College of Arts and Crafts. Art was my first language, and I learned to see the world in terms of color, shape, and texture long before I ever considered what a costume could say about a character. My time in art school taught me to observe, to interpret, and to express—skills that would become foundational when I eventually moved into costume design.

What led you to costume design?

I grew up in Beachwood, Ohio, a suburb of Cleveland next to Shaker Heights, and became obsessed with Millie the Model comic books when I was 7 years old. I sent in drawings, my fashion ideas for Millie, and one of my designs was published in an issue. Under the drawing was the caption, "Designed by Debbie K. Fine." I already considered myself a designer! This was followed by my Barbie phase, which was so intense that my parents bought me a little sewing machine to create Barbie's clothes. My creative productivity overflowed with tiny garments.

    I remember one time, as a young girl, visiting a dress shop with my mother. I found a dress in a child's size made with an imported Italian knit fabric. I sat on the floor with the dress, examining it very closely inside and out. My mother came over and asked me what I was doing. I clearly remember saying, "These clothes feel different, smell different, and they're sewn differently than normal clothes. I don't understand…" My mom sat down next to me and explained the difference between couture and the regular clothing that we buy and wear every day. That was the first time I understood that there was a difference between couture and the clothes that you buy at the department store. I was fascinated by this idea, and that fascination has stuck with me my whole life.

Debra in polka dot dress,
Beachwood, Ohio, 1958.

My mom was very supportive of my artistic endeavors and drove me every week to classes for young people at the Cleveland Art Museum. Another important influence on me was my paternal grandmother. Her home was filled with Chinoiserie, a style of decoration and art that imitates Chinese artistic motifs.

I can't say for certain, but I imagine that these pieces of art, furniture, and rugs were collected in the '40s and '50s—a period that bridged the elegance of Art Deco with the emerging sensibilities of Mid-Century modern. The rugs, in particular, were alive with imagery: birds in flight, peonies (my favorite flower), pagodas, and stylized trees. One rug shimmered in deep jewel tones, another was rendered in softer, muted shades. The vocabulary of those designs stayed with me, and many of my later embroidery ideas were born from those same motifs. The furniture was equally distinctive: a deep, glossy black lacquer, delicately carved, with painted insets and the occasional glint of gold inlay. That aesthetic found its way into many of my '90s designs, especially in the clothes I created for myself. I also remember one large painting that passed down to my parents and hung above their bed. It depicted women basking around a pond, painted in rich but subdued watercolors. What captivated me most, though, was the frame: a wide, black lacquer trimmed in gold. It was decorative and commanding, transforming the painting into something unforgettable. That interplay between frame and artwork has influenced my approach to composition in my own fine art ever since. And then there was the coffee table, a large, round black-lacquered piece with a circular glass top raised about six inches above the surface. There was, of course, no baby-proofing in those days. I can't quite remember if it was me, my brother, or an object that went tumbling into it, but I do remember the drama that followed. The glass went crashing to the ground. I landed on the carpet and those Chinoiserie colors, motifs, and textures wove themselves deeply into my visual memory. They became part of my design DNA—a language of beauty and restraint, where elegance meets imagination.

The Chinoiserie exposed me to Asian design, and when my mother saw the interest that I had in Japanese art, she took me to a gallery in Cleveland called the Verne Collection. Years later, when I worked with James Franco on *Freaks and Geeks*, I discovered during his fitting that the gallery had been owned by his grandmother.

"Reading about Astrology." Painting collage self-portrait by Debra McGuire, 1971.

I was always painting as a child and became more invested in painting and collage in the '60s. It was a tumultuous time. Demonstrations against the Vietnam War pushed me towards political activism and away from clothing design. In college I majored in painting with a religious studies minor. After college, I moved to the Bay Area to paint. That was my first career. I had a studio in the old Shell Oil building in Emeryville and taught painting at the Berkeley Adult School at the University of California. A small San Francisco gallery invited me to participate in a group show where all the artists were required to work outside their medium. I set about creating jewelry, and assembled a necklace made of painted plexiglass and computer chips. The president of I. Magnin, one of the prestigious department stores in town, came to the show and he and his assistant Grace Coddington—who eventually became an icon in the fashion universe—asked me to do a collection of jewelry for the department store.

That's how I transitioned from painting to my second career, as a jewelry designer. The demand for my jewelry exploded. I moved to New York City and started a jewelry company there with a factory in Rhode Island. This success afforded me the opportunity to design a small clothing couture collection. I signed a Japanese licensing deal that led to establishing boutiques that sold my jewelry designs in the Seibu department stores in Japan. I started going back and forth to Japan and the business grew. I was able to hire my talented choreographer girlfriend Wendy Shankin and documentary filmmaker friend Jacki Ochs to help create a video for my company. That was my first adventure in film.

My first costume design experience came around the same time—1985, in New York. Wendy asked me to collaborate on costumes for a theatre piece called *2Tents* for her Calck Hook dance company, which was set in the court of Louis XIV and featured the King, his jealous brother, demented sisters, courtesans, mistress, a jester and a court singer. Wendy wanted white period clothes for all the dancers who would be dancing against a white background. The budget was very limited, enough to pay only a few dollars—or less—for each costume. I hit the streets scouring shops for white petticoats. I took what I found and, inventing as I went along, somehow improvised the petticoats into costumes for the dancers. The *New York Times* review said the piece "offered one sumptuous stage picture after another." My first foray into costume design was a success. In 1987 I got married, had a son in 1989, and since my parents had moved to Los Angeles, we decided to move our family there as well.

Entering Film: First Sets, First Lessons
Transitioning from fashion into the world of film

How did you get into film?

Prior to arriving in LA, I started connecting with people I knew in the film and TV community. Through mutual friends I met with Susan Becker, a well-known costume designer. She was dumbfounded that I would give up a successful jewelry business for the uncertainty and craziness of doing costumes. She knew I had a small child and said that taking on the grueling schedules of working on a film or TV show would be extremely difficult while I was raising my son.

I also spoke to my friend Mark Canton, then Executive Vice President at Warner Bros. He encouraged me to aim for a job as a studio or production executive. I had no interest in doing that, and explained that I saw this move to Los Angeles as an opportunity to pursue my artistic interests. He asked what I had in mind. I mentioned costume design or production design, maybe directing. He suggested that I begin by taking an entry-level production job so I could see up close what everybody does on a film production.

Mark offered me work as a production assistant on the feature film *My Blue Heaven*, starring Steve Martin and Rick Moranis. This opportunity would allow me to observe every part of the filmmaking process, particularly the costume department and the work of the costume designer, Joe Aulisi. I also had the chance to really see what the director, Herb Ross, and the production designer, Charles Rosen, did. Looking back, it was a masterclass in filmmaking, a pivotal experience that sent me into the next chapter of my life.

As I watched how each department in the production operated, it felt oddly familiar. I saw the precision and creativity in Joe's approach to costume and recognized a process that felt similar to the way I had approached designing my own collections. I realized that because of my years working with design teams, fabrics, silhouettes, jewelry and fashion, I already had many of the skills necessary to be a costume designer. I ended up feeling that costume design would not be a big leap but a natural extension of everything I had already been doing.

At the time I was still remotely running my business in New York, so I would come to the production offices on the Warner Bros. lot at five in the morning to call my staff in New York. The crew working on the film were very suspicious of this PA who was always dressed up when the rest of the crew was wearing jeans and t-shirts, and who appeared at her desk early every morning talking on the phone for hours before anyone else started work. They must have thought I was a spy for the studio.

The movie set environment was something I would have to get used to. After years of working in fashion showrooms, design studios, and business offices, there was an informality and congeniality in the film environment—up to and including impromptu back rubs—that did not seem completely professional. The vibe was closer to a summer camp for grown-ups than a high-stakes workplace. People weren't "working" in the way I was accustomed to. In my jewelry business, I had to manage offices in six cities as well as my Japanese licensing deal and a factory in Providence, Rhode Island, where we employed over a hundred people.

Since I needed time for my child and my parents, I thought pursuing a career in LA in movies would be more conducive to the life I wanted to live, rather than maintaining my New York business. In 1987, the stock market crashed and businesses were in dire trouble, which made my decision for me. Of course, film and TV were thriving and not nearly as laid back as they first appeared. Once I committed to making the change, I realized that in this business, like any business, you have to work extremely hard, which I was good at.

How did you get your first job as a costume designer?

As is so often the case with these things, I was in the right place at the right time. I was sitting in a coffee shop in Beachwood Canyon on the east side of the Hollywood Hills in LA and started talking to this woman at the next table. She said she was a production designer working on a Movie of the Week for ABC and that they didn't have a costume designer. I asked her, "Do you think I could be the costume designer even if I've never done it before?" She said, "We've been having a conversation about wardrobe for the last hour and you've done more work with clothing and accessories than anyone I know. You should just go meet with the director and find out." She gave me his name—Chris Thomson—and his number. I threw a resume together just before our meeting. It listed my art exhibitions as a painter and even included things like the fact that I had studied mask carving and pigmentation in Bali, Indonesia in the '70s. Chris looked over the resume and said, "I was in Bali in the '70s"—and from there all we did was talk about Bali. The next thing I knew, he was telling me, "I want you for this job but you'll have to see the producer, Eileen Berg. If you convince her, the job's yours."

I went for my meeting at ABC and was escorted to sit on a couch in Eileen's office facing a big empty desk. Finally, a woman appeared dressed in a sweatsuit.

I thought she was coming to clean the office but she sat behind the desk, looked at me, and said, "Who are you?" I said, "I'm Debra McGuire." She asked, "What are we meeting about?" I explained that I wanted to costume design the movie she was producing. She asked me to tell her about myself. I started talking about my jewelry business and after about a minute she picked up a script and threw it at me. She said "You're hired!" And just like that, I had my first job as a costume designer. The project was called *Stop at Nothing*, starring Veronica Hamel.

At the end of the shoot, the production gave two awards to crew members. One went to the craft service supervisor who prepared the snacks we ate on set, because he was this young kid who apparently had the most creative craft service and accomplished it with a very small budget. It didn't surprise any of us that he ended up becoming an executive at ABC. The other award went to me. It was in the form of a director's chair with the name Edith Keppe embroidered on the back, which is a Yiddishized version of the name of the famous Hollywood fashion designer Edith Head.

When you do a good job, word gets around. This producer recommended me to another producer, George Perkins. He was producing Movies of the Week (MOWs) and contacted me to design one that would be directed by Claudia Weill and shot in Seattle. My son Gavin was only 2½ and I was hesitant to leave home and film on location, but Claudia also had two small boys and convinced me that it would work out and that we would support each other. This film was called *Face of a Stranger*, starring Gena Rowlands and Tyne Daly.

After George hired me for this second job as a costume designer, I continued to work for him on several MOWs. I quickly realized that I could knock them out, one after another. On occasion, I had more than one going at the same time, and one year I did more than twenty movies of the week. They were short jobs: three weeks of prep and four weeks shooting. They weren't profound—a lot were "disease of the week" stories—but each of these jobs produced contacts that led to more jobs. I also got the chance to work with some great actors, many of whom I dressed again on other projects, sometimes years later. Doing those early movies of the week were a kind of trial by fire. I had no idea how to hire a crew and who to hire. And believe me, I made a lot of bad choices.

One of my childhood friends, Dale Pollock, had become a producer and hired me to costume design my first real film. It was called *S.F.W.*, or *So Fucking What*, and starred Reese Witherspoon and Stephen Dorff. I had already worked with Reese on an MOW when she was a 15-year-old child actress, so we had history and adored each other.

I was very fortunate that things worked out like this, but none of it would have happened if I hadn't been open to new opportunities and knew friends who were willing to open doors for me. Experiencing this generosity taught me how important it is to help others as they navigate their own career paths.

Designs of Jennifer Aniston's costumes for *Wanderlust* (2012). Illustration by Lois DeArmond.

Storytelling Through Wardrobe

Characters and their costumes

What is a costume?

A costume is something someone wears that can turn them into something other than who they are. It's something that can disguise, enhance, or help create an illusion.

Why are costumes important?

In film, the job of a costume is to express who the character is visually. We have information in the script that tells us who the character is and their role in the story. But it's a visual medium, so the costume is an important part of conveying the story. Like the dialogue and plot, it's a storytelling mechanism.

Music, dialogue, and lighting help create the mood, but what do costumes contribute to the audience's involvement in the story?

When I read a script, my goal isn't to find a literal expression for what I am reading or even decide what the costumes should look like. I try to get inside the head of the person telling the story and understand what it is that they want to convey to the audience. My job is to design costumes that will support that storytelling. If a costume is wrong or if it doesn't support the story, it can be extremely distracting. The biggest nightmare for a director is to include something in the film that distracts the audience and somehow severs them from the illusion.

When I watch a movie, TV show, or play, the costumes either help me believe what I'm seeing or pull me out of the story and movie experience entirely. Authenticity in clothing is crucial. If a rough, gritty character appears in an outfit that looks freshly purchased, for instance, the illusion breaks. If someone who's been sleeping on the streets for three weeks shows up in a crisp, spotless shirt instead of one that's been aged, dirtied, and sweat-stained, it undermines the reality of the story. It all sounds obvious, but costumes, when done truthfully, really do help audiences stay immersed in the world being created.

Can you give me some examples in your work where the wardrobe or a piece of costume really helped tell the story?

It was when I was working on *Face of a Stranger* that I began to understand how profoundly costume could shape character. Gena Rowlands and Tyne Daly played two extraordinary women whose lives in the story could not have appeared more different. Tyne was a homeless woman living on the streets; Gena was a refined widow whose world had recently come undone. At first glance, these two women shared nothing in common, but over the course of the film, as the two women's relationship deepened, I gradually shifted their wardrobes to reflect that evolution. Gena's refined look softened and became simpler, while Tyne's rough, disheveled exterior grew more polished and composed. By the final scene—set in a graveyard, their silhouettes side by side—the contrast between them had all but disappeared. The vast social and economic gulf that once defined them was gone. That really was the heart of the story: transformation, connection, and the way clothing can express both. What began as mere fabric became a narrative of change, an artifice of costume that revealed something deeply human.

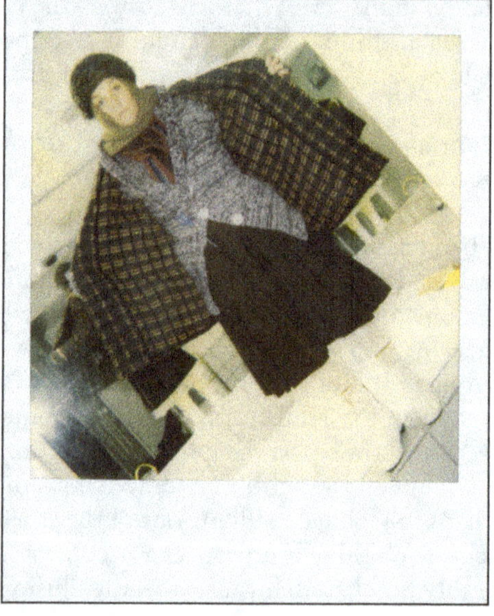

Fitting Polaroids of Gena Rowlands (left) and Tyne Daly, for *Face of a Stranger* (1991).

Fitting Polaroid of Gena Rowlands, for *Face of a Stranger* (1991).

We did Tyne's fitting at her home in Venice, California. I instinctively felt her wardrobe needed to be built from the inside out, starting with the most intimate layer. What would a woman sleeping on the streets put on first, closest to her body, before piling on layers of protection? I remember sitting cross-legged on the floor, surrounded by concentric circles of clothing, choosing what would be the first layer, the second, and the next. Through those choices, I was building her world from the inside—the unseen life beneath the surface. Each piece carried its own history: a shirt once bought new but long worn thin, a sweater salvaged from a thrift shop, everything aged and softened by time and circumstance. The layering became a visual backstory, a tactile record of her struggle and resilience. I did all of this with Tyne right there in the room. With her input as we layered her wardrobe piece by piece she was discovering the woman she was about to inhabit. For a costume designer, that's the ultimate experience: not only helping to create a character through clothing, but witnessing the actor *finding* that character through what they wear. For Gena's role, I designed eleven elegant, Chanel-inspired suits. She loved them so much that she bought them all once filming had ended. It was only years later that I realized how lucky I was to begin my career with actors of this caliber.

Tyne Daly and
Gena Rowlands in
Face of a Stranger (1991).

Another potent example is *Bad Teacher*. The first time we see Cameron Diaz, we immediately understand the essence of her character. She is standing in the doorway of a fairly drab teacher's lounge in a high school, wearing a bright yellow vintage dress. That costume tells us exactly who this woman is and hints at how the story will unfold. The way the dress clings to her body and the bold yellow combine to communicate volumes—without a single line of dialogue. We feel it instinctively. That's the power of costume: it makes us believe, it makes us feel, it defines character before the actor even speaks. What kind of schoolteacher dresses this way?

Cameron Diaz in *Bad Teacher* (2010).

The main character of *Anchorman* is named Ron Burgundy. Director Adam McKay didn't want him to wear the color burgundy, but I insisted. "He has to be in a burgundy suit—he's Ron Burgundy!" There's a scene where Ron bursts through a billboard with his own image on it. I told Adam, "He needs to be wearing burgundy in that shot." Adam wasn't convinced, but he respected me enough to film it both ways—once in a brown suit and another in burgundy. When he saw the two takes cut together, he immediately realized I was right. Production had to build two billboards, and with multiples for suit options, this became an expensive decision.

Certain costume choices don't just support a story—they *become* the story. The burgundy suit did exactly that. Every fan of the movie remembers that moment. It captures who Ron Burgundy is: self-important, oblivious, and perfectly ridiculous. Over the years, that single image has come to symbolize the film itself. That's the ultimate proof of what costume design can do.

What skills does a costume designer need, and what's the best way to learn them?

There are many kinds of costume designers. Some go to school to study, major in and even earn graduate degrees specifically in costume design. My advice to anyone interested in costume design is this: learn to *really see* the world. Open your eyes. Be sensitive to what you observe. Creating costumes isn't so different from painting, sculpting, or studying nature. It's about learning to notice. When you can see and feel those details, you can begin to translate them into character and story through clothing. Learn to see and be curious about what you are looking at.

Ron Burgundy in
Anchorman (2003).

Illustration
by Susan Zarate.

I usually recommend going to art school, where students can learn to under-stand color, shape, and light. But there isn't just one path. Someone might go to business school and gain skills in management and organization, because being a costume designer is much more than deciding what people will wear. It's a large and complex job that requires not only vision, but leadership, budgeting, and strategy. My prior career as a jewelry designer and running a company taught me many of these essential skills.

One of the most important skills is communication—knowing how to express ideas clearly, collaborate with others, and handle difficult personalities with grace.

Designers constantly interact with directors, producers, executive producers, and studio heads. If you can't communicate your ideas and inspire confidence in your vision, it's difficult to bring that vision to life.

When you look at the costume designers who have made a real impact, it's not just passion that sets them apart—it's their work ethic and deep understanding of the craft. Costume design is not simply about sewing or assembling outfits; it's about storytelling. You must be able to read and interpret a script, understand character motivation, and visualize who these people are in the world.

Each medium also requires its own expertise. Costuming for theater, opera, or dance involves entirely different techniques and budgets than film or TV. The garments are often hand-built, intricate, and designed to last through repeated performances. Every branch of costume design presents its own creative and technical challenge. That's what makes the field so endlessly fascinating. Certain film genres require specific strands of knowledge. Superhero films, for example, demand an understanding of specialized materials: how fabrics are engineered, manipulated, and maintained under extreme conditions. I do, however, feel that it is essential to know all the skills—sewing, making patterns and construction—even if you hire artisans to facilitate them.

What's the difference between a costume designer and a stylist?

A stylist is focused on external visual appeal, the surface of how a person presents themselves to the world. A costume designer, on the other hand, begins from the inside out. We're creating a character, a human being with a psychology, a backstory, and a set of circumstances that inform everything they wear. Styling is about crafting an image, a look that communicates personality, status, or taste in a single visual hit. It's about making someone *look* a certain way. There's tremendous artistry in that, but it operates on a different level. It's largely about the *outer* expression of self. Costume design, by contrast, is about transformation. We use clothing to build identity, emotion, and story. A costume can tell the audience who someone is before they ever speak—where they've been, what they want, how they feel about themselves. It's not just decoration; it's psychology in fabric form. When a stylist dresses a celebrity, they're enhancing that person's existing persona. When a costume designer dresses an actor to be a character, we're helping them *become someone else entirely.*

What is the most common misconception about what costume designers do?"

The biggest misconception is that because everyone wears clothes, people think anyone can design costumes. Especially when a show is set in contemporary times—jeans, t-shirts, suits, dresses—people assume, "How hard can that be?" They think it's just shopping. I can't tell you how many times a producer has said something like,

"I saw some blouses at Bloomingdale's that might be perfect for our lead—I could pick them up after work." That kind of comment leaves me speechless, because it reveals a total misunderstanding of what we actually do. Designing costumes—even for a so-called "simple" modern show—is about storytelling, continuity, psychology, and tone. Every choice, down to the texture of a t-shirt or the shade of a lipstick, has meaning.

I once worked with a very well-known director who said to me during a fitting, "Let me take these photos home so my wife can look at them. She has great taste." Imagine the hours of work, research, and preparation that go into building a wardrobe for an entire cast, then being told it'll be run by someone's spouse for approval. It's both funny and humiliating.

Another misconception is that costume design is a glamorous job. It's not. It's a *wonderful* job—it's creative, collaborative, and endlessly interesting. But glamorous? Hardly. We spend our days managing huge teams, dealing with fittings, breakdowns, logistics, budgets, and endless problem-solving. There's nothing glamorous about hauling racks of clothes through mud or sewing until three in the morning because an actor changed their mind about a costume the night before shooting.

And finally, there's this idea that "real" costume design only happens in period films—the corsets, the crinolines, the big gowns. Those are stunning and historically important, but they're also bound by strict rules of accuracy. You're often designing within the parameters of the time, the fabrics, the silhouettes, the methods of construction. In a contemporary project, you have far more freedom—you can invent, juxtapose, and play, but always staying true to the character. You're not necessarily confined by history, but by truth—the truth of the character and the world they inhabit. For me, that's where the most exciting and nuanced design work often happens.

The Interview and Getting Hired
What to say to get (or not get) a costume design job

How do you get a job as the costume designer for a film or series?

After my first few jobs, word of mouth became my greatest ally. People I had worked with recommended me to their colleagues, and soon the offers started coming in on their own. I forged wonderful working relationships with several producers, directors, and showrunners who went on to hire me for many of their projects. At this point in my career, it's about mutual trust and a shared admiration for each other's creative abilities. We've developed a deep understanding from having worked together on numerous projects. But for many years, I did have to interview to get jobs.

When I interviewed for *Anchorman*, I was genuinely excited. The story was set in the '70s, an era that was deeply personal to me. The colors, the silhouettes, the entire aesthetic of that time were part of my lived experience. I didn't need to do research; I had been there. As I read the script, I could already see the costumes coming to life in my mind's eye. For the meeting with the director and producers, I brought a Polaroid of myself from the '70s, standing at the gate of the University of California at Berkeley. I handed the photo to Judd Apatow and his team, and said, "I could do this job with my eyes closed." They burst out laughing, but it was the truth. I didn't have to say much more to convince them.

It also helps to make a genuine connection, to find a point of common ground with the people I'm meeting. Before my interview for *Wanderlust*—a film starring Jennifer Aniston and Paul Rudd, written by David Wain and Ken Marino—my godson, an agent, informed me that David was from Shaker Heights, the Cleveland suburb right next to where I grew up. When I walked in, I was carrying a large manila folder. We chatted for a moment, and then Ken noticed the folder and asked, "What's in there?" "Oh, this?" I teased. "It's my ace in the hole—the reason I know you're going to hire me." I opened the folder and revealed a large-format accordion collage book I'd made titled *Beachwood to Hollywood*, a visual love letter to the creative threads that wove through my life. It was filled with photos, sketches, and artifacts from my journey in costume design, creativity, and serendipity. David flipped through each page, studying the images, smiling. "Yep," he said. "You've got the job. I can't believe you're from Beachwood!" At that point, they didn't even know I'd once lived on a commune in the '70s—the same setting where the film takes place—or that I had already worked with many of the actors in the cast.

How much preparation is required for an interview?

Sometimes I do very little and hope that my reputation can get me the job. Other times, like when I interviewed for *Sonic the Hedgehog*, which I knew would be competitive, I felt it was important to step up and make a splash. Before I went to that interview, I developed a concept for the characters, and focused on the villain Robotnik, played by Jim Carrey. It can be risky to put yourself out there and make a strong pitch for what you think the character should be prior to landing the job, but I had a clear idea of what I wanted to do and organized everything—images and drawings—into presentation boards. I even blew up some images into life-size cardboard cut-outs. I took a big risk, but this was the only design direction that felt right to me, and I wanted to knock the young director, Jeff Fowler, off his feet. Luckily, Jeff was on the same wavelength and I got the job.

But making a big presentation can also work against you. I remember on one project the producers offered me the job prior to meeting the director. My meeting was scheduled at a time when I was still working on another film, so I had access to the art department on that film. I had what I thought were good ideas for the costumes and asked the production designer on the film I was doing to blow up my ideas into beautiful posters, one for each of the main characters. They were spectacular. The film I was interviewing for was a futuristic fairy tale. I arrived with all these posters rolled up under my arm, excited to show the producers and director. The director had just come from Europe and was exhausted. I went into my presentation, but she kept saying things like, "Well, I haven't really thought about the costumes yet" and "I don't really know… I haven't really thought about it." I had done all this preparation and work to create a distinctive look, but the director herself hadn't gone through the script yet or even thought about wardrobe, and I think she was annoyed because I made her look unprepared in front of her producers. I'd never been fired from a job before, but it was no surprise when a month into prepping, on a call with my producer, I was let go. Sometimes things just aren't meant to be.

What should a person interviewing for a costume designer job try to accomplish during an interview?

I want the producers and director to feel confident that I can run a department, that they're not going to have to really think or worry about me, that I have good ideas, and that I know how to facilitate and carry them out. Letting them know that I ran businesses for years is also useful. I think it's important to convey all of this with confidence but without being intimidating.

You want to convince them you have good costume ideas, but they may have ideas of their own. How do you navigate that?

The best way is to demonstrate your ability to contribute but also to collaborate. I've discovered it works best to be strategic about asking the director and producers questions, which hopefully makes it clear to them that my priority is to understand their vision and to design costumes to facilitate that vision. In essence, I'm saying, "If you can clearly express your ideas to me, I can help you realize them." Ideally that's the beginning of a productive dialogue.

Have you ever turned down a job?

Yes, a couple of times, because I didn't want to work with an actor or I didn't want to work with a particular director. Once, in the middle of my interview where I had already been offered the job, I just casually asked if they had hired the line producer yet. They had, and when they told me his name, I couldn't hide my shock. I had worked with him on a film that one of my best friends had written and directed, and he made things extremely difficult for her and the crew. I declined that job.

Throughout my career I have made it a priority to take on work that supported—not disrupted—my family life. I was conscious of the energy I brought home, and never wanted to let the negativity of a difficult set spill into my role as a mother and a wife. From early on, I learned to be selective about the projects I accepted and the people I chose to work with, making sure the experience would nourish, not drain me. I tried very hard, but wasn't always successful. One job I turned down ended up being an acclaimed and hugely successful film. But I had heard horrible things about the director. Maybe I should have said yes, but I'm not sorry about my commitment to protect myself mentally and emotionally, which is another way of protecting my family.

Most of the films I've designed are comedies. I could have gone after big high-profile projects, but this was never a priority of mine. Being in the world of comedy, you spend a good part of the day laughing. When my children became teenagers, I was the most popular mother around. I was doing all the coolest shows and the coolest movies. This was one way to reconcile my not being at home more.

What do you mean when you talk about people or situations being horrible?

There are some directors and actors who talk down to people. For me, the people in my department are part of my family. It isn't enough for *me* to be treated well; I want to make sure my whole crew is treated with respect. It's extremely difficult to make a film with an unpleasant person. I don't care how important they are. I learned early on to steer clear of those who believe in power by intimidation.

Early in my career I was supporting a family, and there were times when I had to say yes to everything. Now it's very different, and these days I only work with people I know and really love. However, there are sometimes things that come up, difficult personalities in other departments, that we can't control and we just have to deal with as graciously as possible.

What role do agents play in getting jobs for costume designers?

Young costumers just starting out often believe that the key to getting work on prestigious projects is signing with an agency. That approach might work for some designers, but my experience has taught me something very different: you can't depend on an agent to build your career. Recently, a costume designer friend told me he had passed on a job because his agent felt it wouldn't be beneficial to his career trajectory. That way of thinking never resonated with me. Jobs led to other jobs through relationships and connections—you simply never know where an opportunity might lead. If you sign with an agent, they should be representing you, your needs, and your ambitions, not shaping your choices to suit their own priorities.

As I said, every job I've ever gotten has come through word of mouth, from the relationships I built—the trust and respect that developed over time with producers, directors, and other creatives. Those connections, along with the reputation I earned through my work, have been the foundation of my career. What I've seen over the years is that most agents are happy to pick up the phone when someone calls them with an offer, but few will go out of their way to advocate for an unknown costumer, to champion them to producers, or to help them land opportunities that wouldn't otherwise come their way. That's the hard truth—especially when you're starting out and no one yet knows who you are.

My friend Stacey Snyder—then a production executive and now one of the most respected leaders in the business—gave me advice that shaped my approach. I was just transitioning out of my jewelry business and beginning to explore costume design. Stacey told me that if I wanted to build a successful career, I should approach it organically. Slowly. Deliberately. "Surround yourself with people you like and trust," she said. "Build genuine relationships. Don't chase the big jobs right away." That advice resonated deeply. Even though I wasn't young and had already run several successful businesses, she made me see that this new chapter required patience—a willingness to let things unfold naturally. The career I was building needed to be sustainable.

For many years, I didn't have an agent at all. I handled my own relationships and used an attorney to negotiate my deals. It wasn't until I turned fifty that a close friend suggested I get one. I signed with someone who, it turned out, was inept. Then I was introduced to Erin Searcy, who was at Gersh at the time and who by now has represented me for many years. Even so, every job offer still comes through people I know and have worked with, though it's Erin who negotiates my deals and looks out for my interests. She understands how I think, how I work, and what matters to me. She is someone I can talk to about work and share my frustrations with. I count on her for the emotional support I often need when working on projects. Occasionally she suggests a project I might go after, but unless it's with people I already know and admire, my answer is always the same: "It's not for me." At this point in my life and career, I choose my work based on trust, mutual respect, and creative connection—the same principles that built my career in the first place.

Designs for *Walk Hard*. Illustration by Anna Wyckoff.

Design and Inspiration

Where a design comes from and how research fuels design

How do you approach doing a design?

I was a painter, and paintings are two-dimensional still images. However, just like in fine art, the costume can be an important element inside the frame. In a John Singer Sargent painting, we can see the importance of the clothes by what the painter is trying to convey to the viewer about the character. That's no different from what we try to accomplish in film, TV, and theater.

Since I didn't have a classic costume design education, I approach design as a painter would. That's why color is such an important part of how I design and why I use color to convey—sometimes subtly—different aspects of character.

For Jim Carrey's costume as Robotnik in *Sonic the Hedgehog*, I started from a character that was created for a video game in 1991. But how do we take that little fat man with the little red coat and the gold buttons and the funny mustache and make him contemporary, interesting, as well as powerful and scary? What occurred to me was to use the lines and angular look of Japanese menswear couture. My designs leaned into a futuristic aesthetic, heavily inspired by Japanese fashion. It was one of the first times I let fashion lead the direction of the design. I watched Japanese runway shows, studied their avant-garde designers, and used what I saw in their designs as inspiration to build out my own concept. I wanted the costumes in *Sonic the Hedgehog* to resonate with the comic book fans who knew the original character because I knew that they were going to be our main audience and critics. After working on hundreds of drawings, I came up with costumes for Robotnik that were approved by everyone. It was a long, arduous process that often felt like squeezing through the eye of a needle. So many strong opinions.

Can you talk about designing for pilots for series?

One of the biggest challenges in TV and now streaming is doing the pilot for a series. The pilot is the first episode of a new series. Networks and streamers often

Left: cartoon image of Robotnik from the 1991 Sega game *Sonic the Hedgehog.*

Right and below: designs for Robotnik and Eggman in *Sonic the Hedgehog* (2018).

lllustratration by Andy Poon.

Left: multiples of
the Robotnik costume.

Designs of Robotnik costumes.

Illustratration by Andy Poon.

Drawing of wedding dress and photo of dress as worn by Catherine Keener
in *The 40-Year-Old Virgin*. Illustration by Angela Carper.

agree to pay for this first pilot episode, and then, if they like what they see, order more
shows or a full series. It means there is a lot of pressure on everyone to make the pilot
great.

Through most of my career there was a period known as "pilot season"—
usually the first couple months of the year—when most of the pilots would be shot.
This would allow the networks to see the finished pilot by the spring and begin full
production for the series in early summer. This was always a very intense, fast-paced
period where I had to hire large crews and come up with complete design plans for a
show in a very short time. At my busiest, I worked on nine pilots in a single season,
but averaged four or five pilots a year. To date I have designed 88 pilots. Producer
Mark Reisman, who I worked with in the mid-'90s, called me his "lucky charm"
because all seven of the pilots I designed for him were picked up to series.

When you design a costume, do you use a computer or do you hand draw sketches?

In the early years, when I was first starting out, I drew all my own sketches, but my union has a job category for costume illustrators and these days they are the ones who draw for me. The sketch artist—or costume illustrator—is an essential member of the costume department. Their work serves as a visual bridge between the designer's vision and the production team. Illustrators are most often hired during prep to help the designer present ideas to the director, producer and studio. Their illustrations can serve as a detailed roadmap if every proportion, seam and design element is clearly articulated. Some illustrators remain involved throughout the production, which can be useful as it allows them to respond to changes as they arise and help develop or articulate new ideas for the designer. They can, for example, incorporate actors' likenesses once they are cast. On fast moving projects I will often bring an illustrator in at completion to document everything that was worn by the principal actors. These "after-the-fact" illustrations help document and capture the essence of the design in a more expressive and interpretive way than standard production stills.

Throughout my career, I have collaborated with many illustrators whose contributions profoundly shaped my projects. Lois De Armond created the original character sketches for *Friends*, helping establish the visual foundation for what became one of TV's most iconic ensembles. In my couture and fashion work, interns from OTIS College, including Angela Carper, produced illustrations that translated my store collections into elegant, communicative images. Perhaps most influential was my collaboration with Anna Wyckoff, whose artistry extended well beyond traditional renderings. Her work ranged from couture sketches enhanced with gold leaf to highly conceptual illustrations for projects like the David Mamet play *Boston Marriage*. These drawings were not merely design documents but true works of art, elevating the practice of costume illustration itself. In more recent years, I have been fortunate to work with two remarkable illustrators, Liuba Randolf and Barbra Araujo. Barbra created drawings for *The Morning Show* and worked with me during prep on *Mayday*. Drawings like these demonstrate the illustrator's practical value beyond design visualization, serving as precise guides for specialty crafts like aging, dyeing, and distressing. When casting is finalized and we know which actors are playing the roles, the illustrator can incorporate their likenesses, allowing everyone—from cutter-fitters to craftspeople—to visualize the garment on the actual performer. This step enhances accuracy, efficiency, and collaboration across the entire costume team. Barbara's illustrations of Ryan Reynolds and Kenneth Branagh in *Mayday*, for example, were especially critical.

What role do mood boards play in the design process and how do you research the images you include in them?

Drawing of period costumes for Geffen Theatre musical production *Atlanta* (2007).
Illustration by Chris Applehans.

I've always kept journals and sketchbooks; they've been a constant companion throughout my life. For me, they're not just a place to write or draw, but a way of documenting how I *see*—a visual record of my curiosity. When I was younger, I created countless collages, piecing them together from fragments that spoke to me— magazine cutouts, photographs, scraps of fabric, bits of color or texture that stirred something inside. It was never just about the image itself but about the *alchemy* that happened when I placed one thing next to another. Those compositions were early exercises in storytelling through image and emotion.

When I became a costume designer, creating mood boards felt like a natural extension of that lifelong practice. It was simply another way of translating inspiration into narrative form, organizing references, textures, and tones to communicate a feeling, a world, or a character. My boards became visual poems, each one a layered map of intuition and intention.

Before the internet changed everything, research was a tactile experience. I spent hours in libraries, pulling heavy art books from shelves, losing myself in images of paintings, photographs, and historical clothing. There were even specialized research libraries inside rental houses like Western Costume in Los Angeles, magical spaces filled with dusty binders of reference photos, fabric swatches, and sketches. You could disappear for an entire afternoon, surrounded by stories captured in cloth. Those archives were sanctuaries.

When digital research arrived, it opened up entirely new worlds. Suddenly, I could take deep dives into subjects that would have been nearly impossible to explore before—obscure periods of fashion, faraway cultures, rare textiles, lost crafts. But even with all that access, I've always loved the *physical* hunt: walking through costume houses, photographing garments, studying the way seams, wear, and age tell their own stories. I still spend hours leafing through art books, not necessarily for costume accuracy but for inspiration—unexpected combinations of color, light, and form that can spark a whole world of ideas.

I've always surrounded myself with visual stimuli. Every workspace I've ever had—whether it's my office on a show or my studio at home—has at least one large pinboard covered with evolving collages of research, sketches, swatches, and photographs. They're like living organisms, constantly changing as ideas develop. I move things around until a pattern emerges, until the story starts to breathe. For me, these boards aren't just tools, they're part of my creative language, a bridge between imagination and realization.

Any tricks that you've learned about doing costume research?

The most important thing is how to go deep. You start on the surface, then dig down deep inside a subject. When I'm researching, I start very broad, looking at general

Mood board for the character of Gilda Radner for *A Futile and Stupid Gesture* (2016).

social and cultural references to the time and place I am researching. I look at the colors that were dominant, how people dyed clothing to get those colors, where the dyes came from, how the fabric was made, how the clothing was manufactured and how it was transported, bought and sold. All these things really interest me.

I recently pulled a vintage dress from a rental house that I wanted to reproduce. By luck, I also found a beautiful fabric that perfectly mirrored the dress's yellow lace. The bolt was wide—about 60 inches—and I thought it would be ideal for the copy. But when I brought it to my cutter/fitter and she took the measurements, she explained that the original fabric used in that era had been created on much wider bolts—about 78 inches. That difference meant that we couldn't make an exact replica. In a workroom, my cutter/fitter and I can usually find creative ways to piece things together, but in this case, the authenticity of the garment would have been compromised. So much has changed in the way fabrics and garments are produced over the years, but when I'm creating a period costume, I always research how things were originally made to ensure historical accuracy. From there, it becomes my job to decide where to honor tradition and where to invent or adjust. One more thing. Finding authentic period garments usually involves meeting clothing collectors and experts focused on that period. So much of what we come up with is the result of the people we meet—many real characters themselves—and garments they tell us about. These relationships we make during our hunt for just the right costume represent a great resource we can go back to whenever we need period costumes.

Is it a special challenge doing period costumes?

As I said, people seem to automatically assume that the biggest challenge is doing costumes for a period film. Period costumes do require creativity and a good eye, but in doing costumes for a period film you're most likely working within the restrictions of what was actually worn at that time and place. Research can be time consuming and it's important to get all the details right, but a contemporary film—which doesn't have these kinds of restrictions—can be even more challenging. Since everyone shops for contemporary clothes, the common attitude is that it is easy to costume a contemporary film. Unfortunately, a lot of producers feel that way too. I think doing contemporary costuming can be complicated and challenging. There are many interpretations of who this character could be. It's up to me to determine the best way to convey this. I often try dozens of options and combinations, and through this process, the character can reveal itself. I then take the best options to the director and we discuss them until we find the best solution. Sometimes, in fittings, the revelation can be surprising or suggest something about the character that hadn't yet been discovered.

Can we talk about your experience working on costumes for period pictures?

Design of outfit with fabric swatches for Christina Applegate in *Jesse* (1998).

Illustration by Anna Wyckoff.

Design of period costumes for *Year One* (2009).

Illustration by Chris Applehans.

I enjoy bringing in outside consultants to help me with specialized costumes or items. Experts can help us to make sure we have accurate spacesuits or medals for uniforms, that kind of thing. It's always a fascinating journey. I start with images that interest me and broad concepts, then zero in on the elements that will move me towards my goals.

Pulling period costumes from costume houses has its own special set of problems. Many of the costumes in my favorite costume houses were made decades ago and have been worn many times. Angels in London is one of the houses with older costumes, though like Western Costume they have an in-house workroom and regularly repair and restore old costumes. I was at one of my favorite costume houses recently and when I touched the lace fabric on a '30s dress, my hand went right through the garment. A lot of these period pieces need to be duplicated because they aren't in good enough shape to be used as is. But if I find something I want to use, I can rent the costume, take it back to the workroom, look for fabrics that are similar, make a pattern, and create a new version of that period costume. I assume most period shows do their own construction.

Page from research book for *Year One* (2009).

How do you make costumes for a fantasy or science fiction project where you have to create fashion or costumes that don't exist in reality?

That's always a fun challenge. I usually look to fine art for inspiration. A piece of sculpture might have an interesting construction that gives me an idea for a certain type of collar on a shirt or dress. Or I'll see things in art galleries, photograph them, and use those pictures, along with pictures I might already have in my own archive, to inspire a new creation.

Creating clothing from scratch is always the most rewarding. A great example is something I designed that was not actually for a sci-fi or fantasy film but certainly could have been. In the '90s, I was approached to take part in a project that sounded, at first, completely absurd. Ford was about to debut the new Focus, and as part of its marketing campaign, they decided to collaborate with ten designers from across the country to create fashion collections inspired by—and made entirely out of—car parts. When I got the call, I honestly thought it was a prank. "Clothing out of car parts?" It sounded like something from a surreal art challenge. Ford invited us to a dealership to get up close and personal with the Focus. They encouraged us to sit in the car, feel the upholstery, touch the dashboard, examine the trim, and really study the materials both inside and out. Then they asked us to submit a list of what we'd like to work with. My request list was as follows:

> Leather from the seats—6 yards
> Windshield wipers—24
> Rearview mirrors—at least 26
> Floor carpeting with all padding and matting
> Seatbelts (black)—40 feet
> Exhaust pipes—2
> Airbags—20
> Microfiber seat fabric, black—6 yards
> Metal Ford Focus insignias—4

When the boxes arrived, they were enormous—filled with industrial materials, metallic smells, and great possibilities. I set up my workspace like a sculptor preparing to build something completely new. This wasn't fashion as I had known it; this was closer to engineering, alchemy even—transforming hard, functional objects into something soft, expressive, and alive.

I worked one outfit at a time, approaching each as a self-contained art piece. I remember taking the tires to a special effects fabricator I knew and asking him to cast the tire treads into wearable rubber forms. Together, we transformed those heavy black strips into choker necklaces and bracelets, then I added diamonds, setting them delicately into the grooves of the rubber. It was the perfect marriage of grit and glamour. One dress was constructed entirely from rearview mirrors, each piece angled slightly differently so that as the model walked, the reflections shifted and shimmered, scattering light like sequins. Another look was woven entirely out of black, glossy seat-belts, a modern take on armor that felt both industrial and elegant.

Left: design of the Seat Belt Dress and a photo of a model wearing the dress during the Ford Focus Fashion Show (2001).

Illustration by Anna Wyckoff.

Below left: Rear View Mirror Dress. Illustration by Anna Wyckoff.

Below right: Airbag wedding gown. Debra adjusting train.

The true centerpiece of the collection—the show's finale—was a wedding gown made entirely from airbags. I built a corseted bodice with grommets along the seams and layered it over delicate white tulle, a deliberate contrast between mechanical strength and bridal softness. The train, twenty feet long, was composed of interconnected airbags filled with more tulle to give them shape and volume. As the model stepped onto the runway, the lights hit the dress just right. And then, to my delight—and slight disbelief—it worked exactly as I had imagined. The train of airbags lifted gracefully into the air, floating behind her like a cloud. It was ethereal and surreal, like the car itself was breathing life into couture. I'll admit that until that very moment, I had no idea if it would behave as I had imagined. Sometimes you need to leap first—trust your intuition, your ingenuity, and your ability to improvise—and hope that the physics of your imagination cooperate. That night, they did, and the result was one of the most unforgettable creative moments of my career. Would I have taken this chance on a film? No. There are so many support departments that could have assisted me in making sure the train floated through space, just as I imagined it. Here it was just luck and intuition.

Have you ever been involved in doing costumes for a movie that has extensive green screen CGI, or motion capture, and how does that affect the work of a costume designer?

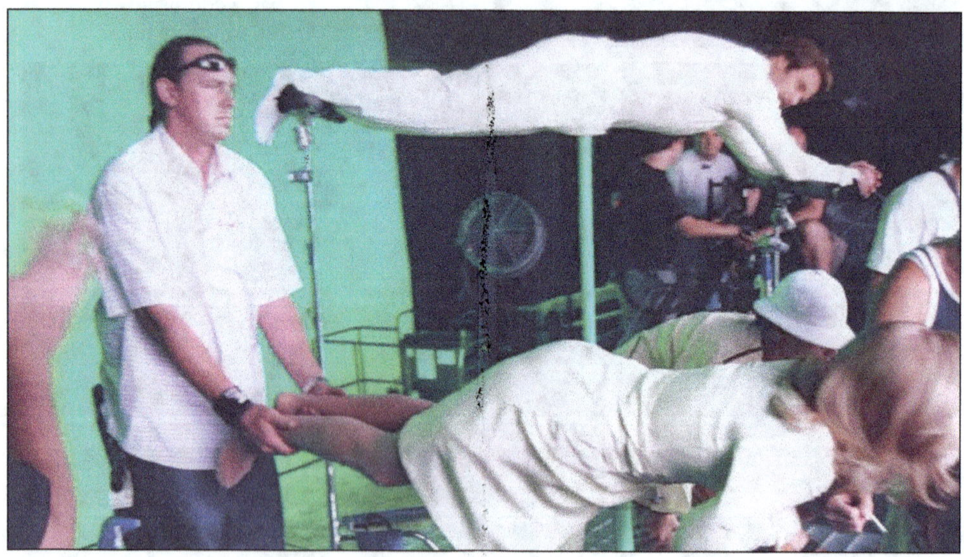

Joe helping characters "fly" while keeping his eye on costume continuity during green screen shot for *Anchorman* (2003).

I've worked on several films and TV shows that involve extensive green- and blue-screen shooting, which has become increasingly common across the industry. These environments create unique challenges for costume designers because the colors we use can directly interfere with the visual effects process. When a production uses a green or blue screen, any costume containing green can disappear or "key out" in post-production. Because of this, I always collaborate closely with the director of photography and the visual effects team to understand precisely which shades to avoid in the costumes we design and make. There are subtle variations. Some greens or blues may still be usable depending on lighting and the keying parameters. We often do camera tests on set, placing garments under the actual lighting conditions to see how they register on camera. Something as common as a pair of denim jeans can suddenly become problematic when working with a blue screen, so we'll test everything, from fabric texture to color saturation before finalizing wardrobe choices.

One of the most interesting technical experiences I've had was on the film *Ted*, where we had an animatronic bear acting opposite a live actor wearing a motion-capture suit. We constantly balanced practical and digital realities, making sure the costumes worked with the physical puppetry, the digital tracking points, and the visual effects that would later bring the character to life. An even more complex challenge came with *Sonic the Hedgehog*, which combined animation and live action in almost every frame. Sonic, the animated character, wears sneakers. When we first see the little speedy hedgehog his sneakers are used and abused, so we had to create a distressed pair, to the point of them falling apart. The sole had separated and needed to be taped together. Later in the story Sonic is given a pair of brand new sneakers, which I designed in a manner that could be produced and manufactured for marketing purposes.

There's also a scene where Sonic rummages through an attic chest filled with real, tangible clothes and pulls out a shirt. I designed and built that shirt first so the animation team could study and replicate its exact texture, drape, and pattern. It was fascinating to see my physical design translated into a digital form that could move, wrinkle, and respond like real fabric.

On projects like these, I've had to learn an entirely new visual language — understanding how costume design interacts with CGI, motion capture, and lighting in virtual spaces. It's an extremely collaborative process that brings together costume designers, digital artists, and technicians from disciplines I never even knew existed when I first began my career. The technology is astonishingly advanced, and working alongside these teams has expanded my creative vocabulary and pushed me to imagine possibilities I hadn't previously considered.

Can you say something about fabric?

Sneaker design and illustration of "Sonic" running in sneakers for *Sonic the Hedgehog* (2020).

Real sneakers that were aged and given to animators for *Sonic the Hedgehog*.

Fabrics have always been a constant source of inspiration for me. When I'm beginning a new project and looking for a spark, I often find myself wandering through fabric stores, walking slowly up and down the aisles, touching bolts of cloth, letting color, texture, and drape speak to me. The tactile experience of fabric—its weight, its sheen, the way it falls or resists—can ignite an entire idea. I've been moved by fabrics so deeply that they have, quite literally, given birth to a costume.

Having spent many years in the couture business, fabric was not just a material—it was the starting point of every story. I bought fabrics all over the world, wherever I went. In Japan, I discovered the kinds of fabric that are used to make obi, richly woven ceremonial sashes, which became one of my signature materials. I used it for linings, under-collars, and hidden interiors—places where a secret luxury could live, even if only the wearer knew it was there. From India, I collected textiles for decades. There was a small mill in Calcutta whose fabrics became an essential part of my collections for over twenty years. I first met their team at the Los Angeles Fabric Show, fell in love with their craftsmanship, and began a relationship that lasted decades. Eventually, I started sending them fabrics I had sourced in other countries—Italian silks,

French cottons, antique trims—for them to embroider or hand-finish. Their work found its way into not just my fashion collections but into many of my film costumes as well.

I've collaborated with mills in Italy, combing through their books of swatches, ordering fabrics to be woven or dyed to specification, and having them produce custom textiles for uniforms or hero costumes. England, too, has been an endless source of fine woolens and suiting. Every country seems to have its own textile soul, and I've always been drawn to finding that essence and translating it into character.

But the fabric isn't just about aesthetics—it's about how it behaves on the body. Some materials are exquisite to the eye but merciless to the skin. When I'm designing for actors, I have to balance authenticity with comfort. Costumes are not just worn for a few moments on the runway; they're lived in, sometimes for sixteen-hour days under hot lights or in freezing weather.

If I'm making a uniform, for instance, the authentic version might be wool, but we'll often make additional versions in lighter, more comfortable materials like cotton. On a wide shot where the texture isn't visible, the actor might wear the breathable cotton version. For close-ups, we bring back the real wool for visual integrity. It's a kind of dance between truth and practicality. Early in my career, I was strict about authenticity. If a period costume required wool, it *had* to be wool. But over time, I learned that honoring the actor's physical comfort is also part of honoring the performance. The actor has to inhabit the costume, not suffer through it. There are exceptions, of course. Will Ferrell, for instance, was remarkably tolerant when he wore a heavy Irish wool sweater for *Anchorman* on a day when the temperature hit 110 degrees. But those moments, while admirable, are the exception rather than the rule.

Sometimes the environment dictates its own version of the costume. While filming *Mayday* in Budapest, we staged a massive parade scene meant to represent Moscow in May 1987. Historical photographs showed everyone in heavy coats and hats. It was cold that year in May. We sourced thousands of authentic wool coats and fur hats for the background performers, but on the day of shooting, Budapest was in the middle of a blistering heatwave. As the temperature climbed, people began to wilt under the layers of wool. At a certain point, the director and I decided to start removing pieces, one layer at a time, to keep the performers safe. We left just enough for the scene to remain believable, even if it wasn't perfectly accurate. Film is always a negotiation between truth and illusion, and that day the heat forced us to choose compassion over precision.

In the end, fabric itself tells stories—about culture, craftsmanship, and character. It carries memory in its weave. Whether it's silk from Calcutta, a coarse Irish wool, or a piece of obi cloth from Japan, each one holds a whisper of the hands that made it. Those textures, those histories, become part of the emotional architecture of the costume—and, in their own quiet way, part of the storytelling on screen.

Fabric shops in India, 2017.

Details from fabrics made
to order in India for use in
Murder Mystery 2 (2022).

Designs for *Vacation* (2015). Illustration by Liuba Randolph.

Breaking Down the Script
Making a practical plan

Can you tell me how you move from the script to planning out the actual costuming for a production?

The script is where everything begins. I do a quick first read in its entirety, primarily to get the story. I read it like a novel. I don't take notes. I don't analyze, I want to be taken on a ride—to feel it, emotionally, intuitively, the way an audience will experience it as a film. My job at that point isn't to break it down, it's to absorb the tone, the rhythm, the emotional arc. That tells me what I need to know about the world we're stepping into.

Then I go through it again, making handwritten notes. I focus on characters and make a list of all the characters. I'll see someone in my mind; not necessarily a specific actor, but the person who lives in that story. I start asking questions: How do they move? Are they guarded? Do they lead with their sexuality or their intellect? What do they carry with them? I'm designing from the inside out.

I read it a third time looking for action and noting any aspects that I need to pay attention to for costume reasons. I go back to my list of characters and write in ideas or impressions I have for each character.

Then Joe, my costume supervisor, will input the script into the program Sync-OnSet, which will generate, scene by scene, details of the changes for each character. If we have a scene-numbered script, the software includes the scene number. Once we have that, we can start thinking about a costume budget to submit to production. Typically, the producer reaches out to us early in prep and will want an approximate estimate of what the costumes will cost. Later in the process we will be asked for a budget with specific totals, line-by-line. A producer will sometimes, but not always, send the studio's initial estimate for a costume budget, but often we start from scratch. Starting with that, we work together and come up with numbers that fit what we actually need to spend, hoping this satisfies the producers and the studio or network. This is a critical point in the process because the producer/studio don't read the script in the same way as a costume person. It's at this stage where we can enlighten them about potential problems, costs, the need for multiples or even potential savings.

Once I have an idea of the actual budget, I'm then ready to have a detailed conversation with the director about the tone of the film, specific shots, that kind of thing, which goes beyond the general character concepts that we have previously discussed. This is when the producer and director try to make production adjustments. If no compromise is made, it might be up to the costume department to find creative solutions to lower costs. This is always challenging for our department. We might involve the first assistant director and try to work together to make things happen. It might be something like reducing the number of takes to reduce the number of multiples needed.

These days, almost everything is shot digitally, and that has changed how we look at color and pattern on camera. When we were shooting on film, there were many ways we could control how color appeared—depending on the type of film stock, the lighting, even how the lab processed it. Each stock had its own character. Kodak film, for instance, gave a warmth to the image, while Fuji leaned cooler and handled certain colors differently. We learned how to use those differences to our advantage. A fabric might look one way to the eye and completely different once it was filmed. Sometimes a pattern that looked subtle in person would vibrate or come alive in unexpected ways once it went through the camera and onto film.

Now, with digital, the camera reads color in a much more precise and literal way. There's less of that film "mystery"—but there are still surprises. Certain colors, especially reds, blues, and whites, can flare or shift under digital lighting, and small patterns can cause moiré—that strange shimmering effect when a pattern and the camera's pixels clash. That's why even now we always camera test any fabric or print that might be questionable. It's the only way to really see how it's going to read on screen in the actual light and environment where we'll be shooting.

The first step is learning about the character we're costuming, but that character doesn't really come to life for me until I know who has been cast in the role. You can speculate and have hundreds of conversations with the director, but it's only once you know who the actor is that things really snap into place. I can't really be sure of what clothes will work until the actor walks into the room and I can see them in person. Before seeing their actual coloring and size, you can't know exactly what will work. That means I have to be prepared with several options, things that are bigger, smaller, even different color palettes. I'm usually sufficiently prepared so that the minute the actor walks in the door for a fitting, I know which pieces will work. But prior to that, I just have to speculate.

When you talk about breaking down a script, what do you mean?

Breaking down a script is basically our way of decoding what the story is going to need from the costume department. As I read, I'm looking for when and where the characters change clothes—how often, why, and what those changes say about their journey.

Once I have a complete breakdown, I can see the scale of the project. How many costumes are required? How many multiples will we need? What's going to have to be built versus bought? All these things give me a better idea of what will be required and how much it will cost. I can also tell if it's what I call a "wardrobe show"—a project with *a lot* of costume changes. On Judd Apatow's *Walk Hard*, for instance, John C. Reilly's character had 118 costume changes over a seven-decade time period. That's a lot of costumes to track. Once the breakdown is done, I share it with the assistant directors so they can plan the shooting schedule with costume changes in mind. It's a roadmap for everyone, showing not just what is needed but how all those details fit into the rhythm of the film.

Polaroid fitting photos of some of the costumes worn by John C. Reilly in *Walk Hard* (2007).

Polaroid fitting photos of some of the costumes worn by John C. Reilly in *Walk Hard* (2007).

Joe

Sometimes I'll get a script before it even has scene numbers, so the first thing I do is number each scene and figure out the story timeline—how many days are there from beginning to end. Then I start building a framework that maps out how all the characters intersect with each other over the course of the story. That's important because it lets us see not only how many costume changes each character has but also who they're sharing scenes with. For example, if two characters who never appear together suddenly meet at a dinner party, we have to think about how they'll look side by side. If they both look great in blue, that's something we have to adjust for. Maybe one changes or we tweak the shade so they don't clash.

By doing this, I get a sense right away of how big the show is going to be—how many changes there are, how much action, whether we'll need doubles or stunt multiples. That gives me a rough idea of the budget. Then I'll talk with Debra and the director to refine it. What are we buying? What are we going to build? How much aging or distressing will be required to make things feel lived in?

By the time I sit down with the unit production manager or the producers, I have a solid picture: the creative needs, the practical requirements, and the numbers to back it all up. It's always a balance between meeting the director's vision, keeping the creative integrity, and staying within the budget.

As I read through the script, I assign script days to the story. For each scene in the script, I ask: what day in the story does this take place? Once I know that the story takes place over, say, five days, I focus on a particular character to see how many of those five script days that character appears. If he has scenes in three of those five days, I know that I may need three costume changes for that character, or maybe, depending on the story, even more than that. Let's say the character goes to a diner, then home, then out to meet a friend, then to dinner with other friends. My breakdown follows that character throughout that day in the story, and my breakdown becomes the foundation for the budget and for my explanation to production as to why I will need ten multiples of that character's blue shirt. Identical copies of the same item are needed to ensure that if it gets damaged or dirty, we immediately have a replacement. The breakdown I do also enables other members of my department to have an overview of the costume changes we need, indicating, for example, where characters' jackets are put on and taken off, where garments need to be aged or cleaned, that kind of thing. There may be a gag in the story—a spill, a tear, blood, dirt, rain, fire—that happens to a specific costume in a scene, and that single moment can radically change what we need to buy, build, or prepare. If a shirt gets soaked with coffee, ripped in a fight, or progressively dirtier over the course of a sequence, we don't just need the shirt—we need clean versions, distressed versions, partially damaged versions, and fully ruined versions, all matched precisely. Those variations must be ready on the shooting day so the director can repeat the action, adjust coverage, or reset quickly without waiting on laundry, repairs, or reconstruction. What looks like a simple visual joke on screen often translates into multiple identical garments backstage, each at a different stage of transformation, and that requirement feeds directly into both the costume budget and the production plan.

I'm working on a film now where I know the filmmakers are drawn to characters wearing printed rock-and-roll t-shirts, so in my breakdown I'm already tracking every instance in which a character appears in a t-shirt that might feature a band. From there, the questions multiply quickly: are we buying originals, recreating them, or designing look-alikes? Do the images require clearance, and if so, how long will that take and what will it cost? Will we need multiples for continuity, damage, or reshoots? All of those decisions flow directly from the initial story breakdown. By identifying the wardrobe requirements at the script stage, I can anticipate licensing issues, production timelines, and budget implications long before we reach the fitting room.

What is SyncOnSet and why is it useful for the costume department?"

It's a production management program that has become an essential tool for us because it's completely interdepartmental. Every department—costume, hair and makeup, set decoration, props—can all work within the same system. We can each do our own breakdowns and still see what everyone else is doing, which is very helpful.

In the wardrobe department, we use it to track everything—our breakdowns, budgets, fittings, continuity. Even if a piece is store-bought, we'll photograph the tags and note the brand, size, and where it came from so we can find it again if we need to. Nothing is left to chance. Once filming starts, we upload photos of the actors in costume, organized by scene number, so we have a visual record of every look. It includes all the details—costumes, shoes, jewelry, accessories, everything—and becomes our working bible, something that's constantly being updated as the shoot goes along. At the end of production, we have this incredibly detailed archive of what was shot and exactly *how* it was shot. That's especially important because, nine times out of ten, there are reshoots. Having that level of detail means we can perfectly match what was filmed months earlier.

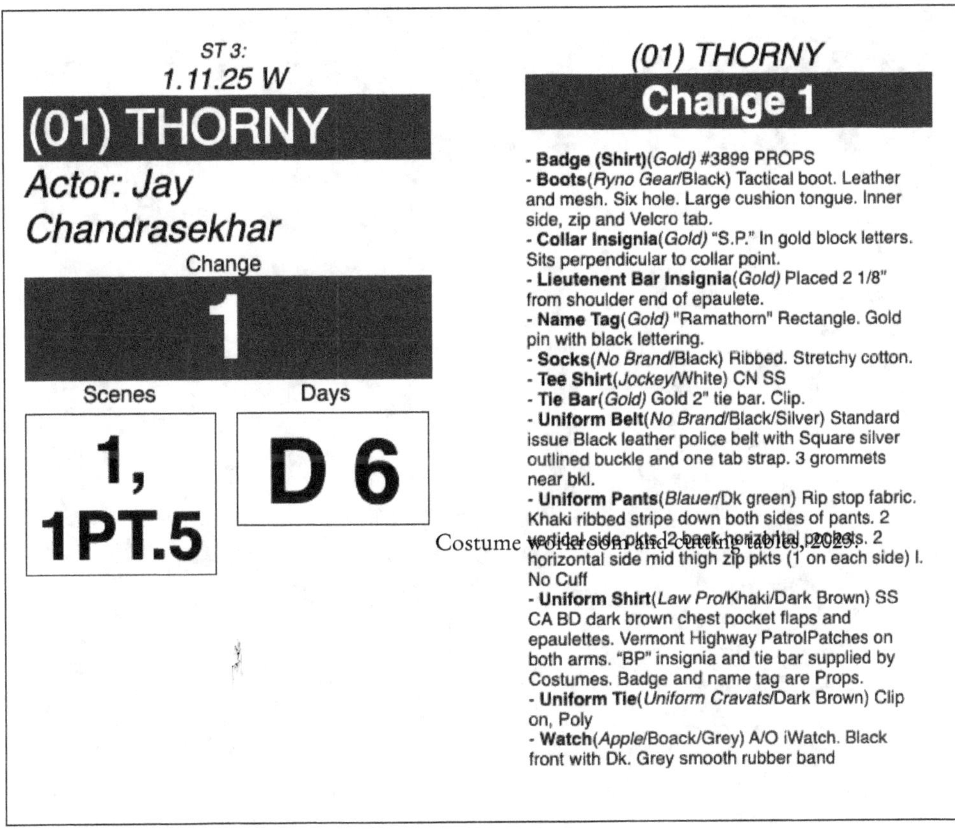

Examples of data on costumes maintained by SyncOnSet for *Super Troopers 3* (2026).

Vintage hat boxes at Circa Vintage Wear, New Bedford, Massachusetts.

Buying, Building and Renting the Costumes
Where the garments come from and how we make them

Where do you get the pieces of clothing that make up the costumes?

Gavin
There are three main places for sourcing costumes in a production. The first is buying clothes, which is the most straightforward and common approach for contemporary costumes. This involves shopping in stores, browsing thrift shops, or ordering items online—essentially the same way anyone would build a modern closet. The second option is making clothes, which tends to be more expensive but is sometimes unavoidable. This could mean printing designs on t-shirts or sweatshirts, creating custom uniforms, or constructing period pieces. It's also the go-to method for genres like fantasy or sci-fi, where costumes need to be entirely original or otherworldly. The third option is renting clothes from costume houses. Many of these have distinct specialties—some focus on uniforms for the military or police, while others are organized by time period, gender, or style. Large costume houses often have aisles dedicated to specific eras or categories, making them invaluable for productions set in the past. Ultimately, for each production, the costume department must decide how every costume will be acquired based on the script, the budget, and the overall creative vision.

Can you talk more specifically about working with costume rental houses?

Joe
Costume rental houses are one of our greatest assets because they carry garments from all periods and things like uniforms which would be very difficult to obtain otherwise. Some costume houses have a lot of uniforms; others specialize in period garments. There's nothing like walking through the aisles of a costume house—you're literally walking through decades of garments. I started out at Western Costume, which was like a living encyclopedia of costume and fashion history.

Palace Costume rental house,
Los Angeles, 2023.

In the old days, every time they built a costume for an actor, they attached a hand-stitched label with the actor's name and the name of the production. As a young costumer working at Western Costume, I remember being excited at finding a pair of jeans in one of the period aisles with the label "Marilyn Monroe." We made sure it was transferred to an archive room where it would be saved as a piece of filmmaking history.

There's something wonderful for young costumers to have the chance to spend so much time in a building where all the eras of clothing are represented. It gives us experience working with all these different periods and different garments, and at the same time, as designers from different productions pull clothing for their shows, we can begin to get a sense of the workflow of different scaled-up or scaled-down shows. The designer would say they need costumes, for example, for a scene in a park in 1965 with X number of women and Y number of men, and as the costume house costumer, you'll pull together a certain number of racks for them to look at and choose from. It's a great opportunity to begin to understand the needs of a set.

When do you buy clothes for a costume and when do you have to create something yourself?

It depends on the project. In TV, when you're doing a pilot for a series, the producers may give you the time and money to have a workroom and create things, but you typically don't have the luxury of having either the time or the money to design and create costumes. The same thing in film. If it's a contemporary film, there might be pieces that we would design and create for the principal actors, and then there might be a portion of the costumes that are shopped.

It all depends on the specific project. For *Mayday*, set in the Soviet Union in 1987, we needed many multiples for certain costumes. In addition to the costumes for Ryan Reynolds and Kenneth Branagh, the stars playing the main characters, we needed copies of the same costumes—multiples—for photo doubles and stunt doubles, sometimes totaling between a dozen and two dozen each. I had to really think about how I was going to create these multiples. We had a workroom and I built most of the costumes for the movie, but for the multiples of those costumes for Ryan and Kenneth, I went to designers like Ralph Lauren and Todd Snyder and looked at men's clothing that would be timeless. There were some pieces of clothing that could have been worn by a conservative man in the '60s, '70s and '80s. I found things like corduroy pants and flannel shirts that hadn't changed for decades. We set up a huge aging and dyeing department and brought in twenty pairs of pants and had the department deconstruct them and make them look lived-in and period. On the TV show *Heroes* we had a workroom and sometimes had to make up to two dozen multiples of costumes that appeared repeatedly in different episodes. We had no choice but to create everything ourselves.

If it's something period and you need multiples, chances are you're going to be building it because you can't find most period clothes in multiples. Tyne Daly's character in *Face of a Stranger* is living on the street and wearing a vintage gown. I realized at some point that a vintage gown wasn't going to survive that kind of rough use, so we created a series of pieces that could be individually stained or destroyed. We took that single gown apart, adding or removing elements as needed from scene to scene. If this had been later in my career, I would have had the workroom create multiples right from the start. Now when I read a script and I know how much money I'm working with, I can quickly determine how much I'm going to build and how much I'm going to buy.

When we build a costume, a specialist pattern maker often comes in, though sometimes the cutter/fitter is also the pattern maker. The people who sew the costumes are very skilled. We shot part of *Mayday* in Montreal, and there I was thrilled to be able to work with a team that was trained at Cirque de Soleil. They are experts in making costumes for performers who need absolute freedom of movement, and they were extremely skilled at putting patterns together. I would bring a couple of them

Costume workroom and cutting tables, 2023.

with me when I was fitting actors so they could do the measurements themselves and see the actual bodies of the people who would be wearing the costumes they were creating. I would walk through their workroom several times a day and observe as the pieces were being created and built. That way I could offer comments on the spot and suggest necessary changes—perhaps the lining or a pocket or belt location. Most of the craftspeople I've worked with—in Los Angeles, Budapest, or Boston—possess an extraordinarily high level of skill. One of my greatest concerns is whether we will continue to have access to people like this in the future. Will young people be willing to spend the long hours at a sewing machine required to develop such mastery? I hope this doesn't become a lost art, because it's essential to what we do.

Joe

Stitching and tailoring can be magical, but most people don't understand that it is really a multi-tiered world. There are tailors and seamstresses who can take a photograph or a sketch and build a whole garment from nothing. Then there are tailors who prefer to follow a very specific pattern from beginning to end. We have seamstresses who come in and clean things up, like hems and quick alterations. If we're doing a big show, the tailors can bring a whole team of people with them. Some will do simple alterations, others build things from scratch. Some tailors specialize in vintage garments, others are expert in building costumes for a futuristic world.

Can you talk about the challenge of dealing with multiples?

Gavin
When planning costumes for a production, the costume supervisor will figure
out how many multiples each costume change might need. That depends on
the script, the budget, and how the costume is used. Sometimes duplicates
are required for stunt doubles who need matching outfits in different sizes.
Other times, the clothes might get wet, torn, or stained, or they need to show
progressive damage throughout the story. To make that believable, we might
create several versions of the same outfit, each showing a different stage
of distress. All of this has to be mapped out early and discussed in production meetings so we know exactly how many "multiples" might be needed to
execute what the director desires. If it's a modern outfit, shoppers—whose

sole responsibility is to purchase or source clothing and materials according to the designer or supervisor's instructions—can buy multiples from stores or online, or we might contact the manufacturer directly. But sometimes the designer or director chooses a specific vintage or one-of-a-kind piece that's hard to replace. In that case, we might find a close match and get approval to substitute it or recreate the garment ourselves using similar fabric and patterns. Once the multiples are made, they are labeled and organized on the costume truck: one section for the lead, one for the stunt double, that kind of thing. Since films are rarely shot in order, your shooting schedule dictates what is needed from day one.

Sometimes we can't get as many multiples as we would like, so the supervisor coordinates with the director, AD, and actor to work around those limitations. For example, if there are only three shirts and one will get ruined in a gag, they rehearse the scene and save the messy take for last. If it's something minor like water or wrinkles, we can usually do a quick fix—dry it off, steam it—and keep shooting.

In the end, it's all about communication. Everyone—from the costume team to the director—needs to know what's available and when, so every look remains consistent and the story stays seamless.

When you buy clothing, as well as jewelry and handbags, do you tend to have relationships with manufacturers or designers or labels?

I've built strong relationships with vendors and manufacturers over the years. Many of those connections started during *Friends*, which ran for ten years. Because it was such a high-profile show, I was able to establish wholesale accounts with almost every major brand, something most costume designers didn't have access to at the time. That experience opened up a whole new way of sourcing for me.

Building relationships with fashion designers is also important, but when I use another designer's work, I can't be obligated to present the garment exactly as it was intended. I need the freedom to make changes—to alter, combine, or reinterpret—so that it best serves the character and the story. That flexibility is essential to what I do. There are times when collaboration with a designer makes perfect sense. For example, if Jennifer Aniston is gravitating toward a particular designer look on *The Morning Show*, I would want to reach out to those designers directly—say, Dior or Saint Laurent—to see the best of what they have to offer for the season.

Those relationships, built on mutual respect and trust, often lead to some of the most successful outcomes. Over the years, I've found that these partnerships evolve much like any creative relationship—based on honesty and a shared commitment to excellence. When designers understand that my goal is to make the character—and by extension, their clothes—look their absolute best on screen, it becomes a true collaboration. That's when the magic happens.

Have you ever worked on a production where, maybe for financial reasons or a deal your star has with a fashion brand, you had to use clothing provided by a specific fashion designer or a brand?

I wouldn't take on a project where the wardrobe is dictated by a fashion house or brand partnership. If the clothes are predetermined, then they don't really need a designer—they just need someone to fit, organize, and maintain what's provided. If a high-profile actor has an ongoing relationship with a particular designer, that's different. In those cases, I'm happy to collaborate and bring in pieces from that designer when it makes sense for the character. But my job is to make all the costumes work together to tell one cohesive story. If I'm forced to use specific clothes in every scene, it throws off the balance and compromises the integrity of the overall design.

Can you give me an example of where you had to manufacture a lot of costumes?

Most of our costumes are made in the workroom of the costume house or studio where we are working. Sometimes the workroom already exists and is being used for other projects on the lot. Most often, we set up our own workroom and hire skilled workers.

There have been times when the only way to achieve what was required was to set up my own production system. On one project, I set up a small factory in downtown Los Angeles, so we were able to produce hundreds of garments for background performers. We ordered rolls of linen and muslin, created the base garments, then sent them to the dyeing and aging teams that we had hired from New York. My earlier experience in manufacturing made this level of organization possible. It was essentially running a miniature clothing industry inside a film production. More recently, I worked on a large-scale sequence that included an elaborate wedding with singing, dancing, and even stunts, meaning we needed multiple copies of every costume for the principal characters and their attendants. There is no store in the world that stocks six or ten identical versions of handcrafted ceremonial garments, so the only solution was to have everything made to order.

I'm fortunate to have long-term collaborators who make that possible. One of my closest partners is based in California and works directly with factories in India. We've collaborated on many productions together, and when it comes to embroidery, fabrics, and color, we truly speak the same language. That kind of trust is rare, and it's invaluable. In this business, relationships like that are everything. So much of what we do relies on them—suppliers, cleaners, rental houses, manufacturers. You can't pull off the impossible without calling in favors now and then. And hopefully, the work and loyalty we bring them continues to pay off in the long run.

Joe

Manufacturing large numbers of multiples involves its own delicate dance of trying to locate everything you need. You need to calculate raw yardage, figuring out how much fabric we need for each garment, then you need to find that amount of fabric, as well as all the zippers, buttons and everything else that's required. It takes a workforce and a workroom, and everything needs to proceed according to a specific timeline. For your average film you get four to six weeks of prep time. Bigger productions need more time than that, maybe three or four months of preparation before filming starts.

You said relationships with manufacturers are important to getting these multiples you need. Can you give another example?

The costumes on *Idiocracy* are a good example of how relationships—and a little bit of insanity—can make the impossible possible. Mike Judge's film is set five hundred years in the future. We were shooting in Austin with hundreds of people. Every single one of them needed futuristic clothing. I remember thinking, *how am I going to pull this off?* I had my guy, The Wiz, in Los Angeles who ran a t-shirt printing company. We had worked together for years on Judd Apatow's projects, and he had become like family. He used to joke that I had ordered so many shirts from him that he put up a plaque in his bathroom that read: "This bathroom was made possible thanks to Debra McGuire." I called him and said, "I need a thousand costumes made from 'sparkle' fabric, used for basketball uniforms in the '90s—asymmetrical, sexy—and every one of them has to be printed with futuristic logos." Without missing a beat, he said, "No problem. I'll just set up a factory in my garage." And he did. He hired people, brought in machines, and started producing the costumes layer by layer. Each logo required seventeen separate color passes—all done manually. It would be easy now with digital printing, but at the time it was a miracle of sheer determination and friendship. Once we solved that, we had to tackle another problem: shoes. What would people wear five hundred years in the future, and how could we get a thousand pairs? I studied everything: motorcycle boots, ski boots, the insides of boots, the liners, but nothing worked for me. I eventually brought in a young avant-garde shoe designer to brainstorm ideas.

Then one day, I'm flipping through a gardening magazine and see these hideous green plastic shoes with holes all over them. I said to Joe, "These are perfect. They're plastic, they're ugly, and they look like they came from another planet." I tracked down the company—they were in Minnesota—and when I called, the owner told me his nephew was working as a PA on our film in Austin. Suddenly, we had a real connection. I asked if he could make them in custom colors—orange for prisoners, red for lawyers. Six colors in all. When I told him we didn't have much of a budget, he said, "Pay me what you can. We'll make it happen."

Prisoner costumes created
in custom orange fabric,
and orange plastic shoes
(later branded Crocs) for
Idiocracy (2004).

A few weeks later, enormous crates of shoes started arriving on set—all different sizes and colors. They were perfect in their awfulness. We started shooting, and a week later, the caterer came up to me and asked if he could have a pair. I said, "Why would you want those?" He said, "Because when I'm hosing down the kitchen trailer, these would be amazing." Before long, every crew member wanted a pair.

Those shoes? They were Crocs! A year later, the company launched and suddenly everyone was wearing them.

Years later, I ran into Mike Judge at a play I designed and asked him if he had forgiven me for using those shoes. He laughed and said, "At first, I wasn't happy—you swore no one would ever want to wear them. But now I get it. Brands take over the world." Exactly the point of the movie.

What role do accessories play in costume design and costuming?

It really depends on the character and the period. I've always loved accessories. I was a jewelry and accessories designer before I became a costume designer, so I have an instinct for using them to express personality. But by the time I started working on *Friends* in the '90s, that era of big, bold statement jewelry had faded. What had once been fabulous—huge earrings, chunky necklaces, dramatic pieces—suddenly wasn't cool anymore. The aesthetic had shifted toward subtlety. Everything became smaller, more understated, quieter. On *Friends*, the only characters for whom I could really use accessories as a defining element were Janice, played by Maggie Wheeler, because her personality called for it, and Lisa Kudrow's Phoebe, because her free-spirited, eclectic nature made those choices feel authentic. For everyone else, accessories had to disappear. They had to support the story, not announce themselves. Accessories are wonderful tools for storytelling, but they have to be used with restraint and intention. When they're right, they can define a character instantly. The shoes I chose for Cameron Diaz in *Bad Teacher* were a perfect extension of her character. They said everything about her attitude and energy before she even spoke.

Where do accessories end and props begin?

At the beginning of every project, I always meet with the props department and go over my list of accessories and the specific items mentioned in the script. It's usually a quick back-and-forth: "I'll take this, you take that." For me, I always want to oversee jewelry, handbags, and sometimes glasses, sunglasses, and watches—depending on how important those items are to the character. I'm fine with the props department handling everyday watches, but not if it's something significant for a main character. Basically, anything that falls inside my *character bubble*—anything that helps define who the character is—I need control of. The union generally decides if items are costumes worn by the actor or if they are props, which means they are carried or manipulated by the actor. This can vary from country to country. On some sets, the props department controls all the accessories. The costume designer gives input, but props and the director have the final say. I saw that difference firsthand when I worked on *Mayday* in Budapest and in Montreal. It was just a completely different division of responsibilities.

Can you talk a little bit about jewelry and its importance in your costumes?

I was a jewelry designer for twenty years—both fine and fashion jewelry—so I have a very strong understanding of it. Even though I don't personally wear much jewelry, I'm fascinated by it. I spent years studying it, designing it, and understanding what makes it feel right on a person. So when I'm dressing actors for film or TV, I have an instinct for how to use jewelry to express character. But you have to be careful. Accessories can also pull focus. A bracelet that catches too much light, earrings that sparkle too brightly, or even a watch that glints on camera can become a visual distraction. You always want the audience looking at the character, not the costume. Jewelry can really define a character; it's a subtle but powerful tool. I've often used it to give a costume that memorable finishing touch. I've also learned how careful you must be. Over the ten years I did *Friends*, I became very aware of that balance—making sure nothing in the costume or accessories ever stepped on the joke. I would even check with Marta Kauffman, our showrunner, when she reviewed wardrobe for upcoming

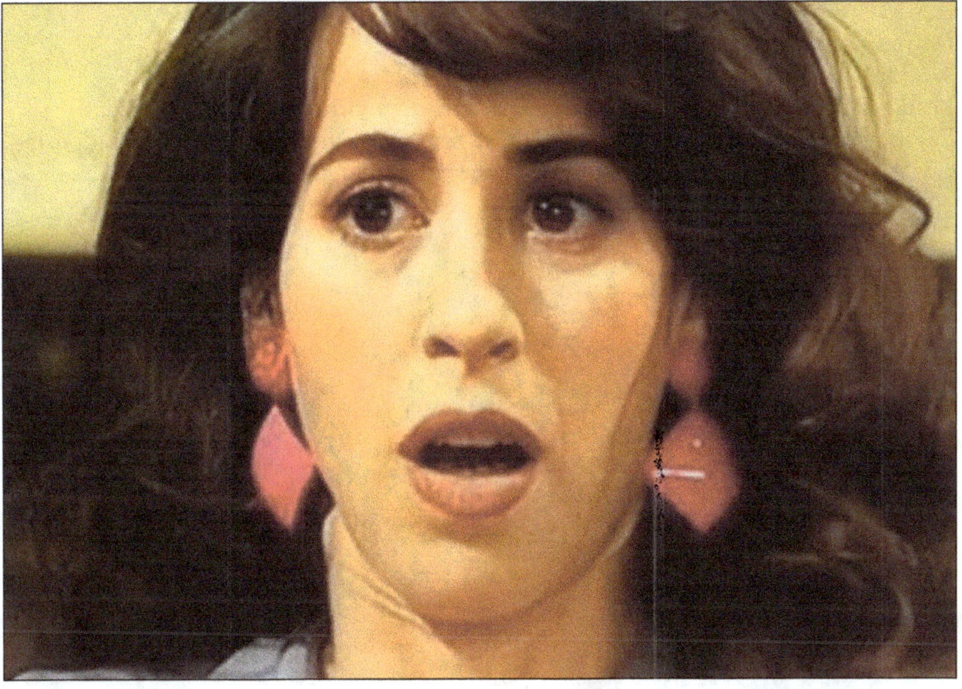

Janice (Maggie Wheeler) wearing pink earrings from Debra Fine Yohai jewelry
in *Friends* (1997). Photograph by Ron P. Jaffe.

scenes, to find out if there were any physical bits or "gags" where I needed to pull back. The fact is that less is often more. At the same time, you never want to miss the opportunity to let a perfectly chosen piece of jewelry help define who that character really is.

What other accessories can be important for a costume?

I already mentioned the Christian Louboutin high heels in *Bad Teacher*. In pre-production, I suggested to the director, Jake Kasdan, that these could be featured early in the film, and he immediately embraced the idea. Whenever I find something like that—a great piece of jewelry, an amazing handbag or a great pair of shoes—I try to find time for a conversation with the director and just say, "By the way, with this outfit, you might want to focus in on this part of the costume if you think it's going to work for the scene." It could be something like a great collar on a dress or, for a man, a necktie, a hat or a pocket square—anything that can immediately project something important about that character.

Do you work much with hats?

I had a hat company in the '80s and partnered with my friend, designer Armand Dirdourian. It was called BOSHI, which is "hat" in Japanese. The problem with using hats in film or TV is that they often cover the eyes. There have been many instances

An elaborate custom-made period hat for *Boston Marriage* (2005).

Oliver Platt as the High Priest in ceremonial headdress from *Year One* (2009).

where I've wanted to use a hat but I've been asked to remove it. On *Freaks and Geeks*, I found a stocking cap that I thought was perfect for James Franco's character but I got a note from the studio that I was taking away from his good looks by putting him in that cap. They thought that he was too handsome to be in a stocking cap. Hats are great for building a character, but they can also be problematic. In my theatre work I used hats extensively. For *Boston Marriage*, I hired a young milliner in LA who was able to articulate my crazy ideas into reality.

Designs for Rachel McAdams, Kyle Chandler and Jason Bateman in *Game Night* (2018).
Illustration by Liuba Randolph.

The Team: Who They Are and What They Do
Leadership, organization and team building

What do you look for in the people that work for you?

First and foremost, they must understand that we work *very* long hours and that every member of the team depends on one another. There's a great deal of responsibility involved, so having a strong work ethic is essential. What we do is a craft, as well as an art. You must have a real passion for it—for the process, the problem-solving, and all the challenges that come with it, and you have to take pride in doing the job well. And, of course, everyone must be a team player. The people who work with me must be able to collaborate, communicate clearly, follow directions, and know how to prioritize.

How do you determine how many people you will need on your crew for a specific project?

After I read the script and have the breakdown, I know how many main characters I need to dress. I can also estimate how many background extras we need for each scene, though I won't know for sure until the first assistant director, who manages the people on set, and the second AD, who manages the actors and extras, let us know. As the production moves forward, the number of background extras usually gets bigger because someone realizes that there are things that the director and the writer didn't initially consider. Once I have all that information, I can figure out what my department needs to look like and how many people I will need.

In practice, the production people have already done a budget before I am hired. It's their estimate of the costume department budget, including the number of people on my crew. But after I have looked at things, I tell them what changes in that budget and staffing they need to agree to. It's always a matter of juggling.

For example, episodic TV can be very challenging because it's very common for different directors to be doing reshoots at the same time a current episode is being shot. When I worked on the show *Heroes*, we had a core crew of about a dozen people. Simultaneous to shooting each week's current episode, there could be as many as five directors on the lot from previous episodes doing reshoots, and each of those reshoots needed an additional costume crew, so my base crew of a dozen could go up to 35. Every day there was a reshoot, I had to scramble to find up to twenty additional crew. I eventually had to hire someone just to do the staffing for the department. We weren't allowed to make that a permanent position. The way that the rates are organized, for every permanent employee, the production has to pay a weekly rate plus the cost of fringe benefits: pension, health and welfare. But if you hire someone for the day, it's a different rate system. They get paid daily, which can amount to a higher total each week than with the weekly rate, but the fringe benefits are much less. I could have a core crew of a dozen and have to staff fifty. That's very complicated. Not to mention that on *Heroes*, we were doing some episodes that took place in the future, some in the past, some were even in feudal Japan or in Russia or India. This was a problem not only for my department but for production design, props, and every other department. Every time they would reshoot, they would have to recreate scenes from those other countries or time periods. This was a huge show that ran for several seasons, with production complications that were consistently difficult.

Joe

You always want enough bodies to get the job done smoothly. On the other hand, it's hard to determine your team until you know what budget level you're dealing with. It's a juggling act, and there's no specific metric. If you're on a modern show and you're dealing with only what is being shopped in department stores, you'll need more people out there shopping in the street, buying and bringing things back, and then returning things, because not everything is going to be used. Many people ultimately weigh in on what costume ends up on an actor. On a period project, by contrast, you may need a much larger team, with people pulling from costume houses that specialize in vintage garments. That requires experienced pullers who are well versed in the period. You'll also need a larger tailoring department because you inevitably find items that are fantastic but one of a kind. At that point, the tailoring team creates multiples in a similar fabric. For this reason, it's difficult to generalize about how many people a project will require. The size of the department is dictated entirely by the show itself. That said, you will always need shoppers and pullers, you will always need a tailoring department—whether you're building extensively or simply altering what you have—and you will also need a dedicated set team. Those are the people who take care of the actors and maintain continuity directly in front of the camera. You have a core group assigned to that work, sized according to the number of actors involved. Sometimes cast members arrive with a specific individual—what we call a star dresser—someone dedicated solely to their care. That then becomes a discussion with production. Who pays? Does the star dresser's salary come out of the manpower budget I am assembling or are they considered above the line and budgeted separately as part of the cost of that star actor? Budgeting for labor is a progressive process. It begins with the first script read and evolves through conversations with the designer and the director, at which point I can determine the scale of the team required to realize the vision. Each area represents a specific costuming category, and the numbers fluctuate across tailors, set costumers, shoppers, and agers or dyers, depending on the needs of any given show.

What jobs and positions make up your costume department?

A group of skilled people each handle different parts of the process. I work with an assistant costume designer, which is a title that covers a lot of ground. On a big film, when there are hundreds of costumes being made, shopped, and rented, my assistant designer is usually by my side during prep. We'll go to fabric stores to pull swatches, visit costume houses, and shop for specific pieces we need. A really good assistant designer understands how I see things—what I like, what I don't—and they work nonstop. They're my eyes and ears, interfacing with the workroom, which they probably created and staffed with the people doing the builds—the ager/dyer team, seamstresses, cutters. They're in fittings with me and keep track of every moving part.

Then there's the costume supervisor. Early in my career, before I had assistants, supervisors did everything—creative and logistical. They handled paperwork, budgets, and timecards, and coordinated where everyone needed to be and when. Today, that role can be divided among several people or supported by costume coordinators, who handle hiring and the enormous amount of paperwork our department generates. The supervisor's job can vary depending on where we're shooting and the local union rules. In New York, for example, supervisors are often truck-based and the job is less creative. Because of the way I like to work, I've always involved my supervisors creatively. Joe, who's been with me for nearly 25 years, started out working on set with his wife when they were both in their twenties. They had an incredible sense of awareness, always anticipating what was about to happen on set. Joe eventually became my supervisor, and he's been an essential part of my team ever since.

Next, we have the key costumers. On a large production, one key might run the set while another oversees the wardrobe truck. They handle the day-to-day logistics, making sure everyone knows what's coming next, what changes have been made, what needs to be prepped. Film schedules shift constantly, so the key keeps communication flowing between the set and the truck so nothing falls through the cracks.

Then there are the set costumers. Each principal actor may have their own, depending on the size of the production. On smaller shows, we might have just a couple of set costumers. On something massive like *Mayday*, we had 55 costumers on set for several days, dressing over two thousand background performers. We also might have a workroom, where we build costumes, and a background department, which can range from a few people to dozens, depending on how many extras are involved.

On certain projects, we hire consultants for highly specialized costumes. On *Mayday*, we had two thousand period Russian military uniforms made in Spain and brought in a military uniform expert to oversee them. We also had period spacesuits built and hired consultants for that. When I do large Indian wedding scenes, I bring in a cultural consultant who understands how saris are properly draped and what accessories are appropriate.

Finally, there are production assistants. We usually have one to three, depending on the size of the show. They handle pickups, deliveries, and whatever the department needs. People sometimes think being a PA is a menial job, but in our department it's incredibly valuable—and a great way to start in the business. You get to see exactly what everyone does and what the work is really like. A lot of people come in thinking it's glamorous, but they quickly see that it's gritty, hands-on, and demanding. If, after that, they still love it, being a great PA can open the door to moving up through the ranks.

What does the costume supervisor do?

Joe

I facilitate and enable whatever costumes the costume designer and the director dream up. Once they articulate a vision and tone, I put things in motion. If we're dealing with a story set in the future, I'll hire a workroom of people that can build futuristic garments for us. If we're doing something modern, I'll assemble a team of shoppers that know the era or style of clothing that we need to find for each character. If it's a period film, I'll help find costumers that know the specifics of clothing or uniforms for that period. I assemble the team and put things into action for our costume designer.

Another way to think about it is that the supervisor is constantly tallying the true cost of creativity. We're always balancing the limits of the studio's budget against what is required to realize the designer's and director's vision, trying to satisfy everyone, which is rarely simple. Often, production hands me an initial budget with some reassuring logic attached. "This will be an easy show for your department," they'll say, "because all the action happens in one day." One day, they assume, means one costume: a shirt, a tie, a jacket. But when I read the script, I see something else. I see the character driving through a crowd, which means an action sequence—and that immediately means stunt performers, doubles, and additional builds. And that's just the start. By the time I've finished breaking down the script, a single character in a single day can require dozens of different versions of the same outfit: clean, dirty, damaged, aged, or adapted for action and photo doubles.

It's never one character, one costume. I always have to think about how the clothing functions and evolves throughout the script.

Can you talk about the role of the costumer on the set?

The set costumer is a crucial piece of the puzzle. They are on set all the time, taking care of the actors and making sure every costume detail is camera-ready. Depending on the size of the production, and if there are A-list actors involved, some performers may have their own personal dressers—people who attend exclusively to them, head to toe. But more often, a single set costumer is responsible for multiple actors at once.

Ideally, the set costumer starts working a few days before filming begins so they can familiarize themselves with every costume and accessory. During prep, we work closely together to ensure they understand how the costumes fit, what accessories go with which look, and how everything is organized. We attach photos to each labeled garment bag so they know exactly what belongs to each character and scene.

Every shooting day begins with the set costumer setting up the dressing rooms: laying out the costumes, jewelry, shoes, undergarments, and anything else the actor needs. If someone has to wear high heels for a scene, the set costumer will hold onto them and swap them out when the time comes, keeping the actor comfortable until the director is ready to roll. They might also carry purses, hats, or jackets—whatever the actor needs for the upcoming shot.

Once the actors are dressed and head to set, the set costumer is always there. They assist with last-minute adjustments, handle quick changes, and help keep the actor comfortable and focused—sometimes even offering water or small touch-ups between takes. During shooting, they watch the monitors closely, staying alert to every detail of the costume. Continuity is a major part of their job. They make sure collars are folded the same way, sleeves are rolled the same, and no jewelry or accessories are missing from one take to the next.

Set costumers are truly the eyes and ears of the costume department. They typically stay near video village, glued to the monitors to see exactly what the camera sees. It's a demanding job—physically and mentally, because they're on their feet most of the day. A character can have ten or more costume changes in a single day. The set costumer handles everything: removing the used costume, prepping the next look, and ensuring the actor knows exactly what to wear in each scene. Sometimes they're right there in the room helping the actor dress, making sure every detail is perfect. Before each new scene begins, I like to have eyes on the actors myself, just to ensure that everything looks exactly as it should before they step in front of the camera. Even once the shooting wraps, the work of the set costumers isn't done. They have to wait until all the actors have changed, then collect, clean, or repair the costumes and prepare everything for the next day.

Joe

The set costumers start their day out in the trailer every morning. We usually have a key costumer on the trailer who works with the set costumer. The costume designer and supervisor bring the garments that will be used in the coming days and the key costumer will prep everything for each day's shooting. Everything will be hung and ready, and we go through everything together, working out all the details: How do we want this garment to be worn? Is the jacket going to be buttoned or unbuttoned? Will the actor even be wearing the jacket in this scene? Do we have specific shoes? Do we have jewelry? Do we have the furnishings we need to keep our actor or actress comfortable?

Then the key costumer hands the garment over to our set costumer, who takes it out of its packaging and ensures everything is designated for the continuity we're dealing with that day. How it's treated depends on the circumstances: if the character has been wearing it for a long time, it may need to look wrinkled; if it's the first time we see the character in those clothes—and the character is neat and put-together—it may need to be pressed. The set costumer has all those notes and preps the costume accordingly. They place it in the actor's dressing room, explain any relevant details, and make sure the actor understands the day's costume changes, then follow them to set. I do what I can to support the team, making sure none of my set costumers is responsible for more than five characters at a time, because one person can only do so much when overseeing multiple characters in a scene.

On set, an important part of the set costumer's job is maintaining that day's continuity. If it's hot, is the actor sweating? If so, will we need multiple shirts to rotate in and out throughout the day? Does some kind of action occur in the costume they're wearing? They may need a clean "beginning" look and then a more distressed version. I might have sent five shirts to the effects department for a scene in which an actor is "shot" and an explosive squib detonates under or near the shirt. The set costumer then has to rotate the actor in and out of these garments between takes—sometimes repeatedly over the course of an entire shooting day.

At the end of the day, all the garments come back to the trailer, are resorted, and the next wave of clothing—the pieces the key has been working on with the designer and me throughout the day—gets loaded into the bay for the following day's filming. The set costumer is focused on maintaining everything happening in front of the camera that day, while the key, the supervisor, and the designer are always thinking a day or two ahead, feeding new garments into the assembly line.

Can you talk about the role the set costumer plays in maintaining continuity?

The set costumer must ensure that the actor is wearing the right costume, in the right way, at the right time in front of the camera. Everything must be prepared and organized so changes happen smoothly and quickly, allowing the camera to keep rolling on schedule. I work from a framework—a breakdown of where every character is going to and from at any given point in the script and along its timeline. The set costumer, meanwhile, stays focused on the two or three scenes behind us and the two or three scenes ahead of where we're shooting. Even on a very hot day, for example, an actor may still need to wear a jacket because two scenes later there's a major stunt and we'll need to hide elbow pads underneath or use the jacket to help obscure the stunt double so the audience doesn't detect the substitution. In the moment, with the actor sweltering, it can be tempting for someone in production to suggest losing the jacket. That's when the set costumer, focused on continuity, has to speak up, ensuring there is no costume lapse that would disrupt the audience's suspension of disbelief and pull them out of the story.

Gavin
A lot of people don't realize that films are rarely shot in the same order as the story unfolds on screen. We almost never start with scene one and move straight through to the end. Occasionally, for stylistic reasons, a project might shoot sequentially, but that's extremely rare. The best hope a costumer has is that the action scenes that impact a character's clothes will be shot in order, but often the shooting order is determined by practical factors—actor availability, location access, and what schedule best fits the budget. Because we shoot out of sequence, it's critical to document exactly what each actor wears in every scene and how they wear it. Was the jacket open or buttoned? How many buttons? Did they remove it mid-scene, or put on another piece of clothing? Every detail matters for continuity.

All this is recorded by the set costumer and entered into a digital catalog that everyone in the department can access, both on their phones and in the trailer. Today, visual documentation is far more effective than written notes, so each costume is photographed in full and in detail—from head to toe. We capture how sleeves are rolled, how shirts are tucked, how ties are knotted, even how worn or wrinkled something appears. Thanks to unlimited digital storage, we can take as many reference shots as needed.

In the pre-digital era, documentation was far more limited. Costume departments relied on a single Polaroid photo per look, supplemented with written notes describing small details. These days, not only do we have instant

Gavin working in the costume tent housing racks of the
custom-dyed costumes for the period extras of *Year One* (2009).

access to digital images, we can also pull exact screen grabs from playback
footage to see how the camera captured the costume on set. This creates
a complete visual database for every look in the film that is available to the
entire department at any time. If we return to a scene for reshoots or pickups,
even months later, that archive ensures we can recreate the precise look: how
the costume was worn, whether it was aged, stained, wet, or damaged, and
every other element of its condition.

After years of doing this work, I learned an unexpected lesson about
continuity during a visit to the editing room. It was a comedy, and the editor
and director were cutting a scene in which the actors were seated at a table. I
noticed that from shot to shot, the glasses were in different positions and the
liquid levels didn't match. So I asked, "How much emphasis do you put on continuity when cutting this scene together?" Their answer surprised me: "None."
With modern digital tools, small continuity errors like that can be fixed quickly
with visual effects—if the budget allows. More importantly, the editor and
director's focus wasn't on the exact position of a glass but on what made the
scene funniest. Still, noticing a mistake can be distracting to a viewer. On set,
much of our work is devoted to maintaining seamless continuity and mini-
mizing those errors, but in the end, filmmaking is about storytelling. The details
matter—but never more than the emotion on screen.

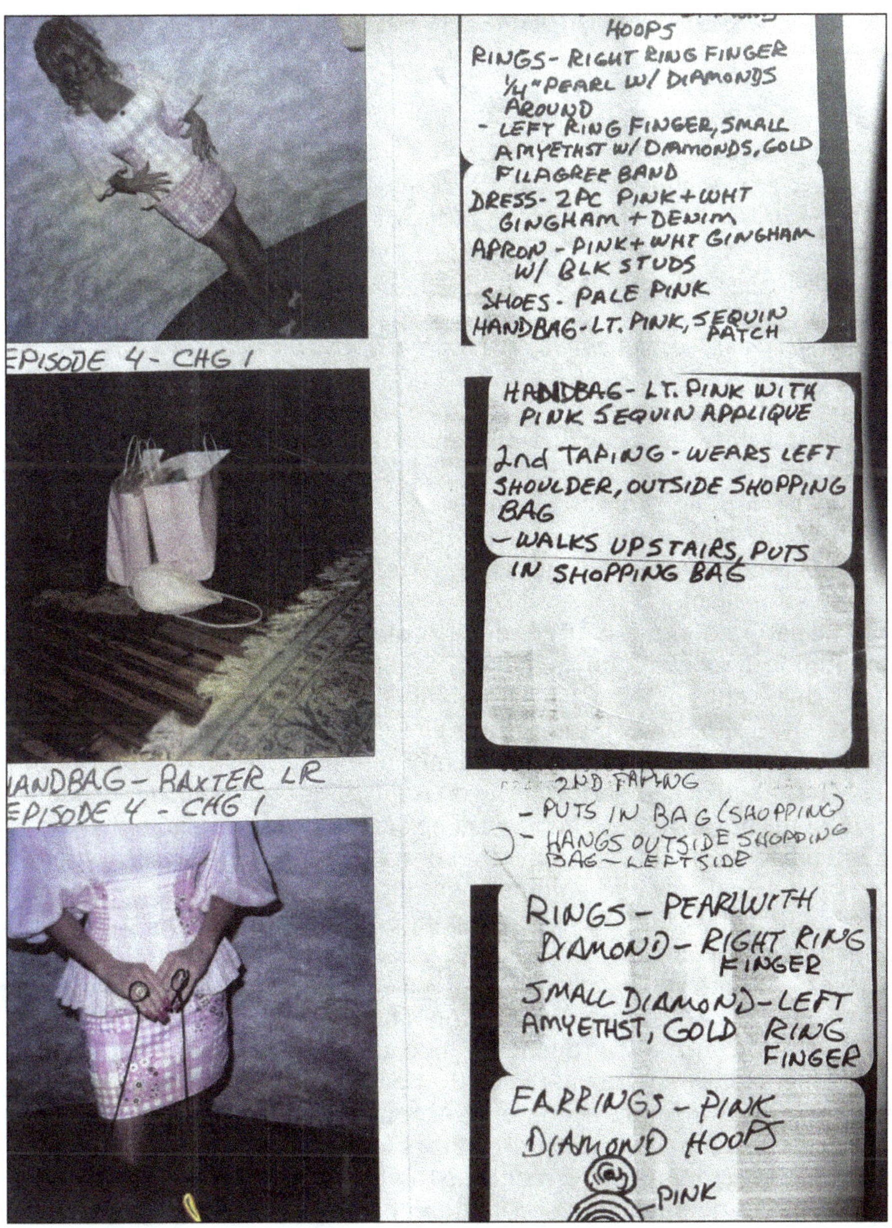

Polaroids of Dolly Parton in costume containing details to maintain continuity for *Heavens to Betsy* (1994).

Is the set costume person is also responsible for taking the wardrobe needed for each scene to the actors' trailers?

Correct—unless individual dressing rooms have been set up at the location. It really depends on where we're shooting. If we're in a hotel ballroom, for example, we may have booked rooms in that same hotel where actors can change between scenes. Sometimes actors dress for their next scene in their own hotel room, and transportation shuttles them to set. But most often, the set costumer brings the costume to the actor's trailer, which is parked near the costume truck, and the actor dresses there.

Can you talk about the relationship between the set costumer and the actor?

Gavin

Every actor is different—each has their own temperament, comfort level, and way of interacting with the crew. A set costumer must develop their own approach to working with actors, and there's no single method that works best. I think most importantly, you have to respect your own craft. An actor will notice whether you take your work seriously, that you move with intention and professionalism.

The nature of our job often requires close physical contact. We adjust collars, smooth wrinkles, pin fabric, or cut off a loose piece of thread—sometimes within inches of the actor's body. Ideally, you are introduced before the first day of shooting, so the actor is already familiar with you. But most often the first interaction happens the moment they arrive on set for their first scene. In those cases, all you can do is introduce yourself, be respectful, and let them know you'll be the one taking care of their wardrobe that day. Depending on the scene, you might need to redress or refit an actor multiple times, or you may only have minimal contact—setting their costume in their trailer, standing by while they shoot, taking continuity photos, and collecting the costume afterward.

We work with actors of all ages—from children to the elderly—and building trust is always key to making them feel comfortable. Some performers don't like to be touched, which can make last-minute adjustments tricky. Others fully understand the costumer's role and give us the freedom to make whatever tweaks are necessary to keep continuity perfect and maintain the designer's vision. Then there are actors who prefer to handle their own wardrobe—tying their own tie, resetting their own shirt between takes—often because they're deeply immersed in their character.

Some scenes bring additional challenges. An actor might be changing clothes on camera or appearing partially or fully undressed. In those moments, they're in a vulnerable position, and the costumer—along with hair and makeup—has a unique responsibility. You're literally touching their skin, so sensitivity and professionalism are essential. Some actors are completely at ease performing shirtless or in minimal clothing. Others need more privacy—robes between takes, a designated changing area, or just a bit of space. It's our job to read that and respect it.

The truth is, every actor is different, every set is different, and every scene presents its own challenges. There is no single formula for how to interact—it's all about reading the room, earning trust, and adapting your approach to meet the needs of both the actor and the story.

Are there things that you try to keep with you or have easy access to on set that you specifically bring to help make actors more comfortable?

Gavin
Every costumer has their own little set kit that they keep close by and that ends up being this mix of sewing supplies, emergency tools, comfort gear, and little things that make the actors' lives easier. Mine contains the basics: safety pins, a lint brush, double-sided tape, sewing needles, thread, scissors, a few quick-cleaning tools for little emergencies. I also keep a larger bag on a set rack for things like a hair dryer, hand steamer, towels, and baby wipes. Actors are often in brand new shoes or high heels that look great on camera but are miserable to wear during twelve-hour shoot days, so we always keep comfortable flats or sneakers ready for them between setups. Sometimes the season in the story doesn't match the real climate we're shooting in, like filming a winter scene in the middle of summer, or vice versa. Having comfort clothes on the set rack—a warm jacket, a robe, or something breathable— helps the actor stay comfortable between takes. At lunch, you want to try and avoid someone eating in their costume, especially if it's a one-of-a-kind piece, so we'll take off their jacket or any delicate part and hang it safely on the rack while they eat. Sometimes I'll hand them a button-up or robe so they can relax without worrying about a spill. Some actors appreciate that kind of care; others prefer to be left alone. It's all about knowing their comfort level. When you're working with kids, that's a whole different game. Snacks, juice boxes, craft services—one spill can ruin a costume or break continuity, so we're always ready with backups, stain treatments, or a clean duplicate if something happens.

You mentioned the aging/dyeing process. That's something I think very few people know anything about.

On *Mayday* we had a team of four to six artists in the aging and dyeing department. For one of the main characters, we built a herringbone wool coat that needed to look as though it had been worn for forty years. To achieve that level of wear, they painted on it, used sandpaper and electric sanders, and bleached and re-dyed sections. The shading of the "wear" created subtle shadows on the front of the coat, with layers of gray and dark tones that gave it depth and dimensionality on camera. For an old, worn sweater the same character wore, they used a small hand tool with a spiked wheel to create realistic pilling. We also needed holes in very specific places, and because it was a knit sweater, the work had to be incredibly precise. One wrong move and the entire garment could unravel. In certain scenes, the sweater had to appear torn, so the distressing had to be carefully planned and executed. And of course, it wasn't just one sweater or one coat—we needed twenty of each, all aged and distressed to look identical. The level of patience and precision required was remarkable. When the producers came to town, I made sure they saw what this team was doing. Their jaws dropped. They had no idea that this kind of detailed, painstaking work went into the costumes for their film. Seeing the racks lined with twelve perfectly aged coats and twenty matching sweaters aged to perfection became a powerful moment of education—an opportunity to show them just how much the costume department contributes to the look, texture, and storytelling of a film.

Gavin

The process of aging and dyeing costumes before they end up on screen is something most audiences might not think twice about. In a Western, for example, you'll see a cowboy in clothes that look convincingly worn—like he's been wearing the same outfit for years. You can't achieve that look with brand new clothes laundered the same day. Typically, clothes are bought new and then made to look old, or we might rent garments that are genuinely aged, find or make multiples that look similar, and distress those so everything feels consistent and lived-in.

Some designers make it a habit to launder all new clothes before they're ever worn, so nothing looks straight off the hanger. And certain actors don't want to wear anything new—they insist that every piece be washed first. From a style and continuity standpoint, laundering new clothes can create challenges. If an actor wears brand new clothes one day and then those clothes are washed before the next shoot, you have to hope they still look the same. Often they do, but not always. For example, if a shirt is 100% cotton, washing it—especially improperly—can cause it to change color, shrink or change shape, which becomes an issue.

Sometimes bright white clothing can be tricky on camera. A director of photography might light a scene a certain way and suddenly that white shirt reflects too much light and distracts from the shot. In that case, we may pre-dye the shirt to give it a slightly yellowed tint so it still reads as white on camera—maybe even as a well-worn white—but no longer interferes with the lighting or color balance.

Another consideration is whether the character is meant to be wearing new clothes in the story. In a lot of movies, clothes just appear—we never actually see the character getting dressed. But when we do, we have to decide how true to life the wardrobe should feel. Does the shirt look like it was recently laundered or like it was pulled off the floor by someone who piles clothes around their bed? Visually, we also want to avoid those telltale signs that give away new clothing: creases from packaging, hanger lines on the shoulders, anything that looks freshly purchased. We'll usually steam or press those out so the clothes look natural and camera-ready.

Actors often have strong opinions about how worn or lived-in their costumes should look, and their input can be valuable. We use the aging and dyeing process not just to shape how the audience perceives the clothes but to help the actor embody the character—like these are clothes their character has truly lived in. Sometimes it's as subtle as roughing up the edges of a t-shirt. Even if the audience never consciously notices, that detail can help the actor embody the character more naturally and deliver a stronger, more authentic performance.

What is the role and significance of the wardrobe truck?

The truck is where the wardrobe lives. They can be quite large—50 feet long and maybe 10 feet wide, usually double or triple racked. Sometimes, if we're lucky enough, there's also room for an office and a washer, dryer, refrigerator, cupboards, that kind of thing. Sometimes we might have a sink and washtub. It depends on the film and the budget. If we also have a background truck, where the background costumer works, then the main truck is used exclusively for the costumes of the principal characters. There is always someone on the truck. When one of the set costumers needs something—a missing accessory, a warming jacket for the actor, something like that—they can call the person in the truck who will bring it right to the set, which might be a distance from where the truck is parked. Sometimes we have the transportation people drive the actor or the set costumer from the set to the truck and back.

Gavin
Once we start shooting, we usually work off the truck. On a big film, we might move items back to an office or studio location at the end of the day and reload the next day, but we usually prefer to have access to all the costumes all the time because we never know when we're going to be asked for something

that's already been shot or need something that was originally scheduled for a later day.

The costume truck is the mobile office of the costume department. We use it both on location and at the studio, usually parked beside the stages or near the cast trailers for quick access to set. Along with most of the costumes, the truck holds essential supplies and a curtained area for fittings. We typically prep the truck a few weeks before shooting begins, loading it with office supplies and everything required to run a small workspace on the go. Inside, the truck has hanging bars running its length. Costumes may be organized by character number or divided by gender—whatever system works best for the team. There's no single correct setup, since we often adapt to local crews and working styles in different states or countries. Characters numbered one through ten are typically the principal cast, each with multiple looks. When a lead actor has dozens of looks, there may not be room on the truck for every costume. That's why coordinating with the truck costumer or set team is important, to ensure that everything needed for upcoming scenes is ready and available. Sometimes this means rotating clothes on and off the truck based on the day's call sheet. Things can get hectic if a director suddenly moves up a scene that was originally scheduled for weeks later. The team might have to rush back to the office, pull the necessary costumes, and get them to set immediately.

On a normal day, the first costumer to arrive at the truck begins to prep the clothes that have been pulled for the day's scenes. Outfits are steamed, ironed, or treated as needed before being set in the actor's trailer. Our truck is always parked close to the cast trailers so that the wardrobe can be easily delivered and wrapped. The set or truck costumer places the clothes in the actor's room and checks that the actor is fully dressed—including small accessories like jewelry.

Throughout the day, costumes are constantly moving between the truck, set, and trailers. When an actor finishes a scene and changes, the previous outfit is collected, checked, and returned to the truck for cleaning, repair, or storage. The truck and set costumers stay in close communication to keep this cycle running smoothly.

Newly shopped or fitted costumes are loaded onto the truck, prepped, and hung in each character's designated "closet." Each costume bag is tagged with the scene numbers it appears in and includes an itemized list of every component. Accessories like jewelry, belts, or ties are stored in labeled mesh bags that hang with the outfit.

Debra on the truck organizing racks for wardrobe changes on the set of
Mike and Dave Need Wedding Dates (2016).

In addition to the tagged, established costumes, we often keep a closet of unassigned or backup pieces for each main character. These pre-fitted garments help the department adapt on the fly, allowing the designer to quickly build a new outfit when a script change or spontaneous decision arises. Some productions also use a separate truck for background costumes—clothing for extras and non-speaking roles. On smaller budgets, however, the background wardrobe must share space on the main truck.

What is the role of the truck costumer?

Gavin

We consider it a luxury to have a truck costumer, and on many productions the set costumers are also required to do the work that would be done by a truck costumer on a bigger production. The truck costumer's job is to alleviate stress and workload on set costumers by making sure everything goes smoothly on the costume truck. They're not there to make any design decisions or to ensure the actor's continuity; they're in a supporting role. The truck costumer typically knows what is coming up the following day and pulls those outfits so we have a good head start. They make sure the costumes are organized and in the right place and that all the items that are supposed to be there are accounted for. They prep them and place them in the truck on the prep rack, which is a place in the truck dedicated to the costumes we're going to be shooting that day.

There are stand-ins for the main cast who come to our trailer for what we call "color-cover." We have a section on the truck with men and women's tops in assorted colors. The truck costumer looks to see what the actor is wearing in the scene and hands the stand-in an item of the same color. They go to set prior to the actors so that lighting and marks can be set.

If certain items needed for that day's shoot haven't been chosen or selected yet or are missing, the truck costumer will get word to the key costumer or designer. They also make note of items as they are being used during the shoot day. They start the process of prepping and organizing the changes for the upcoming day, as well as assisting in setting out clothes for the next day and wrapping clothes from actors' trailers. If an actor or set costumer has gone to set and forgotten something either on the truck or in the trailer, or an actor needs something, the truck costumer will run it over so that the set costumer doesn't have to go and leave us shorthanded on the set.

If a shopper, key costumer or supervisor is bringing anything to the actor's trailer, the truck costumer is available to provide an extra set of hands and help both to load it in and to organize it. They also assist in documenting continuity. In the old days, this meant keeping descriptions, photos and hand-written notes in multiple binders. One set would be with the set costumers at all times, another set would be on the truck. These days we document all this digitally using SyncOnSet, and the truck costumer will help the set costumers log, document and describe every item that is worn throughout the production. The truck costumer is part of the team making note of how each item is worn, the brand, size, where we bought it, all of which results in a comprehensive catalog of everything that the department has for that shoot.

What's the job of a PA in the costume department?

Gavin
You're basically an extra pair of hands to keep everything running smoothly. On a union production, there are strict rules about what a PA can do. They're not allowed to handle the clothes, shop for them, prep them, age them, or manage them with actors. That's because PAs can't replace union jobs. Most of your work as a PA is supporting the department in other ways: picking up and returning clothes, managing receipts, organizing the office, handling paperwork, making supply runs, or delivering anything the department needs. A lot of it is determined by what the supervisor needs at that moment.

What role does the union play in all of this?

My union, the Costume Designers Guild 892 enters into agreements with each production that regulates our working conditions—hours, turnaround, job descriptions and restrictions—as well as how we are paid. They make sure we get paid for overtime, pension, health and welfare and things like that. But they are also our support team. We can go to them with any issues we have with production. We can bring to them workplace problems that result from a situation where we feel that designers, illustrators, and assistant costume designers aren't being taken seriously or treated correctly. They also do things like represent us in negotiations with the industry for new contractual terms dealing with emerging issues that affect all designers, like the use of AI in the industry or payment to designers if a studio or production makes a deal to merchandise the clothing we design.

Gavin
I'm sure for some people their union helps get them work. I haven't had that experience, but I haven't ever pursued work through the union. Each of the local chapters of the union works a little differently. As you move up in classification to a higher role, union rules dictate higher base pay, which is where

I see the union having its biggest impact—that and protecting our rights as workers in the union in addition to providing for our pension and healthcare.

And what qualifications do you need to get into the union?

Gavin
There are a few pathways to joining the costume union. One common route is working in a costume house. In Los Angeles, for example, there are several major costume houses, and working a minimum number of days—typically thirty—can qualify you for union membership. These positions aren't easy to get; many houses have waiting lists, and some may require a year of employment to accumulate those thirty recognized days. Working in a costume house is a great way to learn prep work, fittings, and other foundational skills, though it only covers part of what costumers do on a production.

Another route is through accumulating work experience on set. Prospective members can be placed on the Industry Experience Roster by completing a specific number of union-covered workdays. For entry-level positions, one pathway is achieving a hundred days of relevant work within three years, often as a non-union costume PA or assistant on union productions. Even non-union work can count if it's with a signatory company or performed within the U.S. Once enough qualifying hours are accumulated, a candidate can be sponsored for union membership.

After meeting the experience requirements, the process generally involves contacting the local union to confirm eligibility, completing a membership application, paying initiation fees, and potentially attending an in-person interview. Approval is then granted by the union's membership committee. Geography plays a role too; members must join the local that corresponds to their location and craft. Networking and industry relationships are also critical, as having professionals vouch for your work can make the process smoother. Once you're in the union and maintain your dues, you can work on any union production, although to qualify for benefits like healthcare, you need to maintain a minimum number of workdays each year.

Actors' Fittings and Working with Actors
To become costumes, garments need actors

What role does the actor play in your costume design process?

I'm not dressing mannequins. I'm designing in collaboration with living, breathing artists. Sometimes a costume looks great on the rack but dies the minute someone puts it on. Other times, it's the actor who unlocks the piece—you put something on them, and their body shifts, their face lights up, and suddenly... you see the character. I live for that moment. It's a kind of alchemy.

Can you talk about the importance of the fittings and how that works practically?

I usually like to do the first fitting with the actor alone, whenever possible. Bringing in a full team—your cutter/fitter, assistant designer, and PA to help handle the clothes— can make it harder to establish a personal connection. That first fitting is important; it's where you begin to build trust and open communication. It's as much about listening as it is about presenting your ideas. I never want the actor to feel that I'm imposing my vision on them. I want it to feel like a collaboration, and that's easier to achieve one-on-one, where there's space for an honest and personal dialogue.

I also never make any final decisions in that first fitting. It's just about exploration—seeing what works and what doesn't, discovering the actor's energy, body language, and coloring. I'll pull pieces from the rack and try different things, paying close attention not just to how they look but to how the actor *feels* in them. At the same time, I'm keeping the conversation going, learning about them as a person— possibly where they grew up, whether they have a family and maybe getting a sense of what's important to them.

This can help me understand who they are beyond the character, which can also help with the direction I take with the character. It can also help to relax and distract them from the intimacy of the moment. I can tell almost immediately whether the actor is open to this process or not. It's important that this interaction doesn't cross personal boundaries. Being sensitive and respectful is crucial. Establishing a personal rapport can make future fittings more efficient and even more creative. When the actor and I connect with the character, that energy can find its way onto the screen—and when it does, it's a real win for the entire team.

After I've done some initial exploration, I bring someone in to photograph the actor in the clothes. Those photos are invaluable—they let me see proportions, camera presence, and the subtle ways fabric and color read on film. You can't always gauge those things in person; the camera tells a different truth.

Of course, not every fitting happens in a vacuum. Sometimes the director insists on being there. That can be challenging—once I had a six-hour fitting where the director stayed the entire time—but it can also be extremely productive. When the director is present, decisions can be made in real time. The actor, director, and I can discuss the costume together, refine ideas on the spot, and get everyone's approval in one sitting. That's especially valuable on a TV pilot, where the pace is relentless. Once the pilot begins shooting, it's like a rocket taking off—there's no time to go back and forth with drawings or redesigns. Having those collaborative decisions made right there in the room can get me way ahead of the game.

Are you always at the fittings personally?

Because that personal connection with the actor is so essential—and because you can only truly see how clothes move and feel in person—I make it a priority to be present whenever possible. When I was doing *Game Night*, I couldn't make it to a principal actor's fitting, so my assistant designer Megan went in person while I joined virtually via FaceTime. I had already set up the fitting room and briefed Megan in detail on every look. He walked in dressed like a cowboy. My vision for his character was the complete opposite: cutting-edge, wealthy, sophisticated—a man with impeccable taste. I'd never seen him play that kind of role before. Then he pulled out a navy suit, white shirt, and burgundy tie… and I squirmed. It was too conservative, too safe. "Come closer to the camera," I said. "I need to talk to you." He leaned in. "I see you as this slick, confident guy who has everything—and dresses like it. I know this isn't something you've played before, but humor me. Let me take a shot. I promise I know what I'm doing." He smiled and agreed. Megan pulled out my favorite look—slim, modern, slightly daring. The pants were narrower than anything he'd ever worn. He put them on, looked at himself in the mirror, ran his hands through his hair, and then—right in front of us—transformed. He *became* the character. That wasn't the first time I'd witnessed that kind of transformation in a fitting, but it was the first time I'd ever done it over FaceTime.

Have you used the fittings to convince a doubtful actor to accept your costume choices?

Definitely. A well-known actor showed up for his fitting at Universal looking like he had been on a bender—disheveled, cigarette dangling from his lips, eyes bleary. As he stepped into the fitting room, ashes dropped to the carpet. He rifled through the clothes I had pulled for him, unimpressed. "Yeah, I don't like any of this," he muttered, his energy restless and defiant. Every time I tried to take his measurements, he squirmed away, making the process nearly impossible. Somehow, I managed to get him into a blazer and a pair of slacks that fit—though he made it very clear he didn't approve of them.

Still, as frustrating as it was, that fitting gave me absolute clarity about his character. I saw it in an instant. Despite his lack of cooperation or interest, I knew I could give him a costume that would help create the character. I designed with a specific palette in mind: crisp white pants, a powder blue blazer, and snappy blue ostrich shoes—courtesy of a buddy in downtown LA—plus a few more outfits in the same vein. I didn't show him the clothes until the day he was shooting, but as soon as he tried them on it was as if a switch flipped. Suddenly, he was a different person. After that, every day I went to the set, I got a hug from him.

The first fittings for *Sonic the Hedgehog* took place at Jim Carrey's home in Los Angeles. We started with more conservative street wear, as requested by the executive producer. I had brought a lot of John Varvatos to cover that base, but to me, it felt all wrong. Thankfully, I had also packed some Japanese avant-garde pieces—just in case. Not surprisingly, Jim balked at the conservative looks, so I pulled out the hidden stash. When he put them on, something clicked. It was obvious to us both that this was working and his character started to emerge. But now I had another problem: how was I going to explain this to the producer? It was a long and tedious process getting everyone on the same page.

Can you talk in more detail about how you deal with actors during their fittings?

Actors come from all kinds of backgrounds and enter the business in very different ways. Those who were trained in the theater generally have a deeper understanding and respect for costume work than actors who began in film or TV. You can always tell the difference. When we go to their trailer or dressing room at the end of the day and find that everything has been carefully hung up, organized, and ready for the next morning, we know instantly: "That's a theater person." By contrast, it's not unusual to walk into a trailer and find the wardrobe piled on the floor. That tends to happen more often with younger actors, and it's not always their fault. Many of them simply don't realize what's expected. They've never been told. But for the set costumers who take care of those clothes—who work long hours making sure everything is clean, pressed, continuity-correct, and ready—it's disheartening and feels disrespectful.

I've been on shows where, with the producer's support, I've called a meeting with the entire cast to explain exactly what the costume department does. I tell them that their wardrobe doesn't magically appear; there's a team behind them, working incredibly hard to make them look good in every scene. And I remind them that while they may have private bathrooms in their trailers, the costumers must often walk a long distance to use a honey wagon. It's a small thing, but it illustrates the difference in privilege. The point isn't to shame anyone—it's to build awareness and respect. Once actors understand what goes into supporting them, most are genuinely appreciative and more considerate moving forward.

Have you had actors who don't want to go to fittings or were too busy for them?

It's rare to find an actor who *enjoys* fittings—especially when we're building a wardrobe from scratch and need them to come back multiple times. Most actors tolerate the process, but few look forward to it. There have been some fabulous exceptions. John C. Reilly was the most enthusiastic on *Walk Hard*, a film in which he wore dozens and dozens of different costumes.

When I started *Friends*, I imagined building all the costumes for the six characters, but it quickly became clear that wasn't realistic. We simply didn't have the time for that many fittings or the schedule flexibility to constantly bring actors back every week for alterations.

On some projects, I've developed creative ways to minimize the number of in-person fittings. One is by creating a custom body form that replicates the actor's exact shape. We take their measurements during the first fitting, build a form that mirrors their body, and then do the subsequent fittings on that form—bringing the actor back only for the final check once everything is nearly finished. When I designed for Dolly Parton, whose schedule was nonstop, we had a mannequin made to her exact proportions. On larger films, when the budget allows, I've also hired professional fit models or body doubles. These aren't the same as stand-ins who work on set for lighting or blocking. Fit models are cast specifically because they share the actor's exact measurements. I can fit them as often as needed, make all the adjustments, and then call the actor in only when everything is ready for a final fitting.

Early in my career, before I realized I could hire body doubles, I sometimes used myself as the model. On *Anchorman*, Christina Applegate and I happened to be the same size, so everything was fitted on me first. Christina came in only at the beginning and end of the process, and all her costumes fit perfectly. Later, when I dressed her again for *National Lampoon's Vacation*, I knew she wasn't a fan of fittings, so I took a different approach. I did all the shopping and preliminary styling using a fit model with her measurements. We photographed every look—head cropped out—for the directors to review and approve. By the time Christina arrived, everything was ready for a quick, efficient fitting, which she appreciated.

Gloria Chan (cutter/
fitter) pinning the
Robotnik costume
onto Jim Carey, for
Sonic the Hedgehog
(2018).

There are always ways to make the process easier. Actors' schedules are relent-less, and respecting their time is important. With experience, I've learned to anticipate their needs, streamline the process, and make fittings as painless—and productive—as possible.

How do you prepare for a fitting?

Gavin

Multiple people are often involved in the process. Beyond the designer, there could be shoppers, the key costumer, the supervisor. For each fitting, we organize a rack of clothes—or sometimes an entire room of racks—depending on how many looks or changes a character requires.

When working with a principal actor during prep, there may be multiple fittings to help build a consensus around the character. Often, the actor has only a vague idea of who the character is, and stepping into the fitting room filled with different concepts and options based on the designer's vision can help them define the role. Occasionally, actors will have their own ideas about what their character should wear, and if we know that in advance, we try to have those options available. But generally, the process is guided by the designer's vision and how the clothes fit the actor. Tailoring and alterations are done as needed to make everything look as good as possible.

Building a character's costume can involve taking hundreds of fitting photos. The costume designer will sort through them to select the ones that best articulate their vision. These choices are then presented to the director and may require additional approval from the network, showrunner, or producers. The goal is to home in on a cohesive look, creating a progression that shows the character in everything required to tell the story. This is why it's essential to have a wide range of options available at the fitting.

Fittings for day players—actors who may only appear in a single scene—are different. If a character is a doctor, for example, you're not necessarily shopping for hundreds of dollars' worth of clothing. Instead, you follow specific instructions from the designer, providing just enough options for the scene: a shirt, pants, a lab coat, and photos of the actor wearing them, images which help the director make an assessment. The goal is to have as many looks and photos ready as possible so you don't have to call the actor back for multiple fittings.

Once you have these photos, you can start building a vision board or a progression of outfits for the character. It's critical to read the script carefully for practical limitations. If a scene requires a character to put something in their jacket pocket, for instance, a look without a jacket obviously won't work. Costumes must be functional as well as stylistically appropriate, supporting both the character and the specific actions they perform in each scene.

I imagine with certain famous stars it can be difficult to arrange time in their schedules for fittings. How do you manage that?

Fitting Polaroid of
Michael Cera for
Year One (2009).

Fittings with major stars are scheduled far in advance and coordinated through their assistants or representatives as part of their daily calendar. For *Mayday*, I flew to England with my assistant designer, Martine, to do fittings for the two lead actors, Ryan Reynolds and Kenneth Branagh. Because their schedules were so tight, we had to bring a large selection of garments with us. Those initial fittings were extremely important—they allowed me to see what worked and what didn't. Once I completed the fittings, I had a clear sense of direction. I photographed each look, then reviewed the photos with the director to confirm what he responded to before moving forward with orders, multiples, and new builds. To streamline the process, I also hired doubles with the exact same measurements as the actors. That way, we could continue refining the builds in their absence.

For *Mayday*, we were constructing vintage spacesuits. Precision and authenticity were everything. When I went to England, we already had one completed suit, which I brought for the fittings so we could make final adjustments directly on the actors. That suit became our model for the additional nine or ten that had to be fabricated. Because parts of the suit were made from metal, I flew in the craftsman responsible for those components so he could be on-site to ensure every detail fit perfectly. We only needed to bring the actors back for a few follow-up fittings. Everything else we handled on the body doubles.

And what about the ongoing relationship between the costume person and the actor?

That relationship can be wonderful—or challenging—depending entirely on how comfortable the actor feels with what's happening. I've been very lucky in my career; I haven't had too many difficult experiences. But when things do go wrong, it can be tough. There's simply no excuse for bad behavior, especially in a fitting. It's such an intimate and vulnerable space. If you can believe it, I've had male actors—including one very famous one—show up for their fitting not wearing any underwear.

When someone crosses a line early on, I address it immediately. I'm not afraid to set boundaries—firmly but calmly. It can make things tense for a moment, but my goal is always to defuse that tension and create trust. If the actor isn't comfortable, they can't give their best performance. In a way, it's psychological work as much as creative work. Being a good costume designer often means being part artist, part diplomat—and part therapist.

Early in my career, I had a well-known actor behave terribly toward a member of my team. My set costumer came out of the actor's trailer in tears because the actor had thrown his dirty socks at her. I walked straight in, stood in front of him, and said, "We need to be clear about something. You are lucky to have this wardrobe department. But if you humiliate anyone on my crew again, we will walk. Have I made myself clear?" He looked at me and said, "Yes, ma'am." Twenty years later, I still run into him occasionally, and he always tells people, "This is the woman who put me in my place." Many years prior to becoming a costume designer, I taught in a junior high school—and honestly, the film industry isn't all that different. There are a lot of people who behave like adolescents, assuming they can be dismissive or demeaning just because they have power. I've never tolerated that. I will always stand up for myself and my team.

Sometimes, though, it takes strategy—not confrontation. I once had to design for an actress with a reputation for being very difficult. I imagined her character wearing spectacular, expensive jewelry and thought that if I gave her something that made her feel truly special, it could shift the dynamic. I convinced the production to let me borrow millions of dollars' worth of real jewelry, complete with private security and insurance. When she came in for her fitting and saw the jewels, she lit up—and from that moment on she was a dream to work with. It worked for her as a person and for the character she was playing.

Any experienced costume designer will tell you that research is key. I always talk to other designers. I'll look up an actor's last project and, even if I don't know the designer, I'll call them. Not because I expect to have the same experience—every relationship is unique—but knowledge helps, especially when it comes to body image or physical sensitivities. If an actor has certain insecurities, I like to know in advance so I can prepare and maybe have the right support garments ready without needing to discuss it. This applies to both male and female actors. These are the kinds of small things that can make a big difference,

In the end, what it comes down to is respect—mutual respect—and a shared goal: helping the actor become the character. That's how the magic happens.

Gavin

After a long shooting day, an actor might toss their costume around as they undress, or take home the jewelry or other small costume pieces. They may think it's no big deal, but efficiently wrapping a room and returning all items is critical. Sometimes we only have a limited number of specific socks or a single piece of jewelry. If an actor doesn't return them, it can create serious problems for continuity or future scenes. Clear communication with the actor regarding their process and yours is essential for the department to run smoothly. Having a conversation with an actor regarding your needs as a costumer can go a long way in building that mutual trust and respect. Depending on the situation, sometimes the conversation about handling costumes properly needs to come from someone with more authority, like the costume designer.

You can learn a lot from how an actor handles their costume at the end of the day. When we first set out their wardrobe, everything is generally pressed or steamed and organized on hangers in their dressing room. This can include pants, shirts, socks, shoes, and accessories like bracelets, bandanas, or jewelry. Some days, we may have multiple changes laid out. If the actor strips everything off and leaves items scattered, it takes extra time to track everything down. This can not only strain my relationship with the actor but also impact the department's efficiency and our ability to turn the wardrobe around for the next day. Sometimes I might need to stay late so I can wash and prep the clothes, often under pressure from the production office to finish quickly and avoid overtime.

Joe

When they are playing a role, actors are trying to become someone else. As they should be, they are focused on the fictional character they are creating. As costumers, our focus is on the material things that fictional characters will wear, so we have to stay rooted in the real world, and in a way the costumer is the actor's anchor to the real world on set. It's an essential role. We step into the actor's space while they are focused on their character and, without disturbing their focus, find a way to adjust how something is buttoned so that it looks the same way it did in the last take. And between takes the actor needs to be able to know that you're standing there with a coat when it's freezing cold or a robe to cover them when they're only partially dressed and vulnerable. As soon as the director says "Cut," we're right there to assist them when they transition back from playing a role to being an actor on a busy set. It is a delicate relationship, and some set costumers are better than others with actors one-on-one. Others are better with large groups of actors. It's about pairing people up whenever and wherever you can so that they succeed together.

Are there special challenges dressing the guest stars who make an appearance for an episode or two on a series?

It depends on the actor and the show. The goal is to help the actor understand the character. It might mean that you make them look less attractive, which is always a challenge. Sometimes it can be very easy. When Julia Roberts was a guest on *Friends*, I went to introduce myself, knocked on her door, and found her lying on the couch in her dressing room. "Any idea what you'd like to wear in the scene?" I asked. She looked me up and down and said, "I like what you're wearing—let me try it on." I stripped off my black velvet button-up shirt and matching pants. She slipped them on, twirled around, and said, "This is perfect!" "Done and done," I said.

It was a little more complicated when Brad Pitt was a guest star on *Friends*. He arrived for his fitting and tried on what I had pulled, but Brad had a lot of his own ideas. I listened, shared my thoughts about the character, and agreed to pull some of the vintage pieces he requested from Palace Costume. I knew they weren't right—but I also knew he'd see that for himself. I photographed him in each option, and we sat down together to review. They made him look like a runway model—exactly what we didn't want for the character—and when he saw that, he quickly agreed to wear one of the outfits I had originally chosen for him, cleaner and preppy.

When I designed *The New Girl*, we learned that Prince was going to guest star in an episode. He apparently had a crush on one of our stars and saw the show as his way in. I contacted his people to find out how we should proceed. Would he prefer us to pull the wardrobe for him or would he be more comfortable wearing his own? I was told he'd be bringing his own things but that we were welcome to gather a few options as well. I headed to Palace Costume and pulled some fabulous pieces. I also reached out to a few designers I knew. We gathered a great stash of options for him. When he arrived, entourage in tow, it was surreal. Prince was smaller than I'd imagined—tiny, really—and his feet were size 7, the same as mine. He brought some incredible boots, including a pair with heels that lit up. We dressed him in a mix of our selections and his own. What struck me most was how oddly normal it all felt. I was sitting in a director's chair when he came over and sat beside me. We started chatting— about Minnesota, the weather, our teen years. He was soft-spoken, gentle, and funny. At one point he walked over to the couch and just started strumming the guitar.

Do you have any style, tricks or routines you have developed that have helped you develop a personal relationship with actors?

Gavin

It's beneficial when you're able to meet an actor before their first day on set. They're often coming into a production where everyone else has been working together for weeks, so the costume department may be the first crew they meet. Having a brief conversation in the costume office or during a fitting allows you to introduce yourself and start building a relationship before the cameras are rolling. If that isn't a possibility, an introduction at base camp, before they arrive on set, is preferred.

When helping an actor with their costume, it's important to be hands-on without being overbearing or distracting. Some actors enjoy chatting casually, while others need to stay fully focused on their lines and performance. You have to be aware of their needs and adjust your presence accordingly.

It's also valuable to explain what you need to do for your job. For example, when an actor finishes a scene, I might say, "I'm going to need continuity photos—a full-body shot and a few detail shots of the costume. When's the best time to take these?" Later, when shooting is faster-paced, I check in: "Is this a good time for costume photos?" Some actors don't want to pause between takes, and in those situations you have to be sensitive, sometimes needing to take photos via the video monitor rather than asking the actor to stop. Making sure the actor understands why these photos are necessary for continuity helps them cooperate and makes the process smoother.

Understanding the production as a whole also helps build trust. If I see a shot where an actor's shoes won't appear on camera and I know they're uncomfortable because maybe they're brand new, I might offer to swap them for something more comfortable. Anticipating needs like this shows the actor that you're looking out for their comfort while staying aware of the larger production.

Actors notice and appreciate the little things—running between takes to grab a warming jacket, keeping them dry, or adjusting something so they're more comfortable. We're not just standing by; we're there to support them and make their work easier, and that attention to detail goes a long way in developing a strong, respectful relationship.

Can you talk about the relationship the costume department has with background actors and how that is different from your relationship with the principal actors?

Gavin

Some extras only appear briefly in one scene, so you don't build much of a relationship with them. However, there are background actors who recur across multiple scenes or episodes. Over the course of a production, you may get to know them and even build a small "closet" for a core group of recurring extras—characters associated with principal actors who never speak. Some of these actors make a career out of background work, auditioning for speaking parts while regularly appearing as extras on different productions.

Most background actors are new to you each day. They typically arrive earlier than principal actors because we need to get them dressed and the ADs need to place them on set before filming begins. Background actors can create unique costume challenges. When a scene requires extras, our department often drafts an email, sent by casting, asking them to bring clothing that fits the scene. When they follow instructions, it's great—but often they don't, and we have to scramble to find something appropriate. For scenes like Westerns, sci-fi, or military settings, we have to supply their costumes and hope everything fits comfortably for a long day of shooting. Occasionally, we have the luxury of bringing in background actors for fittings days or weeks ahead, which ensures the outfits fit correctly. However, this is expensive. Most of the time, extras show up on the morning of their shoot and we have only a few minutes to establish rapport. Building that relationship, even briefly, is crucial so they follow instructions and maintain continuity—keeping jackets on, buttons done up, clothing in the right position—throughout the day.

Even though extras may only appear in the blurred background, it's our job to monitor them for continuity. A positive working relationship makes this much easier. Early in my career, I sometimes saw background actors as a necessary nuisance. Over time, I've realized that treating them with respect and building rapport goes a long way. Besides the ADs and hair/makeup, the costume department is often the crew they interact with most, so fostering good relationships ensures smoother cooperation and better results on set.

Joe

Whether there are dozens of background players in a crowd scene or a handful in the background of an intimate dinner, our background players are an essential part of convincing the audience of the reality of our story. For a daytime shoot, we tend to meet with our background artists at 4:35 AM in the morning. I like to think of our large costume trailer as "a closet on wheels" which is filled with garments in advance of a shooting day. Our department will send all the extras in each scene a short note of the kind of clothes we want them to bring with them to the set. They are unaware of the tone or look we're going for, so in addition to what they bring with them we have numerous garments in the trailer we can use to dress them correctly for their scene. Often, despite our advance instructions, what they bring with them doesn't work for the scene.

When the extras first show up for their scene, it's a bit of an adventure. If we are going to have to dress 15, 25, or even 200 background artists, I will schedule extra costumers for that day just to deal with the extras, since our set costumers will be busy dealing with the principal actors. While the set costumers are usually near the camera and can hear the first AD and the DP discussing details for the next shot, our background costumers are much further away and typically will not hear those bullet points. Often, they arrive on set only when the ADs bring in the background extras and won't have much time to assess exactly what the camera is seeing so they know which of the extras will appear most prominently in shot and can give them appropriate attention.

As the day progresses—and we sometimes have *very* long days—the extras might get relaxed about their costumes and leave items in the background holding areas. This means that additional costumers taking care of these background artists may have to work hard to maintain continuity. Since they have so many people to watch over and none of them are stars, it can be an exhausting and thankless job. When the camera pans across a crowd of people in winter jackets and there's one guy who got hot on set and took his jacket off, it can really throw off the audience's belief that the scene is taking place in wintertime—despite the reality that we're shooting that scene in the middle of summer.

Can you talk about the difficulties created by having to dress a large group of background actors?

It's crucial that the background is dressed correctly. It's our responsibility to ensure that every extra looks exactly as we want them to look. Their costumes must never distract or interfere with the audience's focus on the principal actors. Color plays a huge role in this. Making sure the leads stand out visually against the background is as much about palette control as it is about style. Typically, we do "lineups" where the background actors stand in costume and I walk past every one of them with the director, scanning for anything that needs to be adjusted or replaced. Even when we were dressing two thousand background actors on *Mayday*, my team and I checked each uniform for accuracy, down to the placement of every braid and medal. It's meticulous work, but essential for authenticity.

Of course, when you're dealing with many extras, there is always the potential for chaos. Our experience on *Year One* was particularly challenging. We were shooting in the middle of New Mexico, far from the pool of professional background actors you might find in Los Angeles or New York. Many of the locals hired as extras looked as though they had been pulled straight from the streets—or, in some cases, out of jail. We had to cover or camouflage tattoos, sometimes from head to toe. One day, a police cruiser and a paddy wagon pulled up and hauled several background players off to jail, still wearing their biblical costumes. Apparently, drugs were being passed around and some of the extras were prostitutes working in costume. It became the ADs unenviable task to wrangle them all each morning and somehow turn that motley crowd into a believable ancient civilization. On another day, while shooting in town, several extras vanished. The ADs eventually found eight of them sitting in a bar, happily drinking, in full biblical regalia. By the end of each shooting day, we honestly wanted to burn the costumes. We couldn't, of course—but more than once, we had to throw pieces away. Everyone on the costume team wore plastic gloves, though sometimes even that wasn't enough to keep us clean.

Set costumer adjusting details on the uniforms of background extras, 2023.

Pages from Debra's notebook for a film that never happened: a Janis Joplin biopic.
Illustrations by Maggie P.

Budgeting

Our wardrobe is shaped by how much we can spend

Who does the actual budgeting for your department and how is it done?

Once we have the breakdowns, my supervisor and I create a preliminary budget. We start by estimating what we think the costume department will need, then go through it in detail with the Unit Production Manager (UPM) and line producer—the people responsible for managing the overall production budget and approving expenses. We want them to fully understand how and why we arrived at our numbers. Sometimes, our proposed budget comes in lower than what production anticipated. On a recent film, for example, there was an Indian wedding sequence with a large number of costumes. My previous experience designing Indian weddings helped me to find a cost-effective solution without sacrificing authenticity or visual richness.

Reaching an agreed-upon budget can sometimes be challenging. The process works best when there's trust on both sides, so that line items can be adjusted as we move forward to cover the inevitable surprises: last-minute costume additions, unexpected script changes, new creative requests from the director. Without that flexibility, the job becomes extremely stressful. There's nothing worse than knowing you don't have the money or manpower to do it properly. Still, I've learned over time that once production is in full swing, things tend to loosen up. Resources shift, priorities become clearer, and somehow I've always been able to get what I need.

For example, if a project includes a large number of principal and background actors but the budget only allows for two set costumers—which I know is insufficient—I'll immediately communicate that to production. We can then make a strong, reasoned case for adding crew. Joe is especially skilled at explaining exactly what's required and why, which will often make the difference.

This is where clear communication and smart negotiation are vital. The costume designer and the supervisor must be able to advocate effectively for the department—using logic, experience, and practical business sense. Every request we make must be backed by solid reasoning, because the UPM and line producer will, in turn, need to justify it to the studio executives, who control the purse strings. If we present a strong, well-substantiated case, we almost always get what we need.

How do you know how much things are going to cost?

First, we decide which pieces will be purchased and which will be built in our work-room. The cost for building in-house is determined by how we configure our labor budget. To some extent you have to guestimate, but from experience I have become a very good guesser. We also buy a lot online, which has made shopping and pricing easier than it used to be, especially when we're on a tight budget. If we can't afford to build a suit that needs multiples, for example, I can order several different suits online and see which works best. Once decided, we can order however many are required, including, if needed, larger sizes for stunt people, who are padded and so need bigger items, and actors' doubles. The ease of online ordering is a game changer. In the past we had to pound the pavement, scour the city, call connections in other states and countries to ask for assistance and direction. In some instances it still needs to be done this way because a personal connection is valuable and can present new ideas and opportunities.

Joe

I'm always walking through department stores and vintage shops so I can be aware of the cost of clothing and generally what is happening in the industry—which is always changing. We've had some interesting speed bumps over the years. There was a point before the pandemic where malls and department stores were really kind of suffering, the result of which is that many of the major clothing manufac-turers are no longer creating such huge lines. Once you could reach out to any clothing manufacturer and say, "We're making a movie. I'm going to need multiples on this. Can you send me 15 or 24 copies of a single shirt direct from the factory?" That used to be easy. Now manufacturers are making clothes only to fill specific department store orders. X amount of these plaid shirts will be going to Macy's, Y are going to Nordstrom, Z are specifically for small vendor boutiques—and that's it. These days I might reach out to a specific vendor and the typical response is they've shipped everything they have and there is nothing left in the warehouse. That makes our job more difficult. If the vendor no longer has any copies, we need to source the fabric they used for the original so we can build duplicates and multi-ples on our own. It's only with experience that you can be aware of a problem like that and be prepared to budget for it.

Most stores and vendors change their clothing with the seasons. Part of the job is knowing which vendors carry winter attire all year because there will be times when, for example, you're in the middle of summer and need to shoot photos of a family vacationing in the mountains during winter. Or one summer you could be prep-ping an entire film set during the winter. It's just as difficult to try to find a bikini in the middle of winter if you're trying to prep and put together a summer film in January.

Collaboration with the Director

Stories of partnership, trust and on-set problem solving

Talk about the relationship between the costume designer and the director.

It's clearly one of the most important relationships on a film. The director is creatively steering the ship and ultimately has the final say on everything that appears on screen. Ideally, the relationship is built on trust and communication so strong that I can almost read the director's mind and anticipate what he or she wants before they even say it. When I've worked with a director multiple times, I often find myself intuitively knowing what they're going to need, sometimes before they do. That kind of synergy only comes with experience, mutual respect, and a shared creative language. If communication with the director isn't good, it just doesn't work for either of us, so part of my job as a costume designer is to stay two steps ahead, anticipating needs and preparing for the unexpected. That's much easier when you understand a director's personality, taste, and working style—especially if that includes spontaneous or last-minute decisions.

My personal philosophy is *never to say no* to a director. "No" simply isn't in my vocabulary. That doesn't mean everything is possible, but I'll always find a way to get as close as humanly possible. I understand that many costume designers draw a hard line. "We can't do that, we're not prepared." But I've built my career on doing everything in my power to make things happen, even under impossible circumstances. I was working on *Wanderlust*, shooting in rural Georgia—literally the middle of nowhere. It was dusk, around six o'clock, and David Wain, the director, who I absolutely adore, came over and said, "We're thinking of doing a scene tonight where everyone drops acid. It would be great if everyone were in wild, surreal clothes, hair, and makeup." I looked around—there were no stores for miles. I knew what I had on my costume truck and that it wasn't going to give him the trippy psychedelic world he was imagining. But I didn't say no. I said, "Give me a minute. Let me see what I can do."

This was before online shopping existed, so Cathy, the supervisor, and Megan, the key costumer on my crew, jumped in the car to look for *anything*. They stopped at a gas station and asked the attendant if there were any Halloween or costume shops nearby. Miraculously, he said, "Yeah—there's one, it's closed now but I know the owner." He called him, the owner opened the shop, and told them to take whatever they needed and come back the next day to settle up. An hour later, Cathy and Megan pulled up with a car packed full of costumes. My entire crew went into overdrive—ripping things apart, mixing and matching pieces, collaborating with hair and makeup to create the most outrageous, psychedelic looks imaginable. The result was spectacular—completely over the top, wildly creative, and done in record time. And of course… the scene never made it into the finished film. Some of the best costume work we've ever done ends up on the cutting room floor. That's part of the job.

Working with directors like Judd Apatow is a perfect example of why this flexibility is essential. I've done multiple films with Judd, and after a while I could practically anticipate his next idea before he said it. He's an incredibly spontaneous filmmaker—constantly writing, revising, and inventing new scenes as we shoot. On *The 40-Year-Old Virgin*, when we first broke down the script, each main character had about forty costume changes. Judd kept adding new sequences of little moments, and by the end of the shoot, each lead had over ninety changes. We had to pull off dozens of entirely new looks with almost no notice.

Today, whenever I start a new project, I plan for that kind of spontaneity. We always keep a rack of "wild cards"—extra pieces that have nothing to do with the current script breakdown but might save us later. On one show, we even kept a full lion costume on the truck "just in case." With directors like Judd, you never know when inspiration will strike—and when it does, you have to be ready to bring it to life.

Gavin

The relationship between the costume department and the director is essential to bringing a project's vision to life. The stronger that relationship is, the more effectively we can anticipate what the director needs and execute their direction with confidence. As a key costumer, I'm part of early prep meetings where I listen closely to the conversations between the costume designer and the director—how they discuss tone, character development, or shot ideas. Those early insights are what guide our work once we're shooting.

Communication and trust are everything. A director who's clear and collaborative makes it easy to plan ahead, test looks, and fine-tune details, whether it's the exact level of distress on a jacket or how much blood splatter should appear in a scene. We'll often prepare samples, photos, or test garments in advance so the director can approve them quickly, sometimes even bringing options to set between takes.

Every director is different. Some have an exact vision and know what they want down to the smallest detail. Others need to see multiple options before they can decide, which can strain time, budget, and even morale if not managed carefully. In those cases, it's about staying diplomatic—making sure the director feels supported while keeping producers and actors confident in our department's work.

Ultimately, our job is to make the director's vision seamless on screen—to help them tell the story without distraction and make sure every detail, from the costume's design to its condition in a scene, serves that story.

Can you talk about your process in working with a director to figure out the costumes for a movie?

There's the fantasy of working with a director, and then there's the reality. Ideally, we'd have time to sit together and explore every character in depth—talking through who they are, what they represent, and how their clothes can express that. Some directors I've worked with make that time a priority. We'll have an initial meeting, I'll listen carefully to what they're imagining, then I'll go off with my team to develop ideas. Later, I'll return with very specific concepts and visuals to discuss.

But that kind of collaboration is rare. Directors are pulled in so many directions—they meet with every department head—and often there simply isn't enough time, so part of my job is to be prepared to work intuitively, to anticipate their needs, and translate their ideas even when we haven't had much time to talk.

An exception was my experience with Adam McKay on *Anchorman*. It was his first film as a director, and he was incredibly open and curious about the process. He wanted to learn what a costume designer could bring to the storytelling. I told him that if we could go through the film shot by shot, we could build something visually original—something no one had seen before. I explained how we could design not just for individual characters but also create a cohesive color palette and silhouette language that would unify each shot.

If you look closely at *Anchorman*, especially in the group scenes, you can see that the characters' colors and shapes harmonize with each other. That wasn't accidental. We crafted those looks so that when they appeared together, the frame itself became more dynamic, more painterly. I wanted Adam to see that costume design could be a powerful storytelling tool—one that shapes the emotional and visual rhythm of a film. In *Anchorman*, the clothes don't just support the story—they are very much part of the story.

Have you ever had to fight for a design you believed in?

Many times. But you pick your battles carefully and only fight for what you *know* is right. It's tricky, because the full power of a costume choice often isn't visible until you see it on screen, in context, when it becomes part of the larger storytelling.

Judd Apatow and me in '70s costumes, on the set of *Anchorman*.

A more recent example is from *Super Troopers 3*. We had a huge wedding sequence, and the actor playing the groom—one of the leads—is a big guy who needed to move a lot physically. There was a joke in the script about the traditional coat he was supposed to wear. I knew that if I put him in that coat, he'd be miserable and restricted, and the comedy would fall flat. I suggested moving the joke to an earlier fitting scene—where he tries on the coat—and letting him wear a shirt and vest for the ceremony itself. It gave him the freedom to move. The director loved the idea.

Color can also be a battleground. Sometimes directors or producers don't understand how repetition or harmony in color can elevate a scene. They'll say, "Two characters can't both wear blue," but in life, people *do* wear the same color—and sometimes, visually, it's more powerful when they do. I like to imagine the frame from above, almost like an aerial view, to consider how all the visual elements—movement, color, texture—interact. That's when the costume design really starts to sing.

Do most directors really understand what a costume designer does?

Not always. When I first worked with Adam McKay, it was exhilarating because he completely understood how integral costumes are to storytelling. I remember thinking—and I even said it to my team—*I wish every director could understand this.* I wish we had the time on every project to show them how much we can contribute to the overall vision. But the reality is, most of the time, there simply isn't enough time for that kind of collaboration. It's the same with actors. I've worked with some for many years and they still have no real idea what I do. They often only see the part that affects them directly—their own costume—which is understandable and very much the nature of this business, but still frustrating. Film and TV can be very self-focused. There's a lot of ego, and a lot of jockeying for power. Being a costume designer sometimes means navigating all that quietly while still doing everything you can to serve the story.

What's the biggest lack of understanding or misconception?

People who aren't in the industry usually have no idea how much work it takes to make what we do look effortless. Our goal is always to make it seem easy, to do our job so seamlessly that it never creates a problem for anyone else working on the film. The ideal is that the director, producer, or actor never has a single negative comment about the wardrobe department. Whatever challenges arise, we keep them to ourselves. Maybe we're *too* good at hiding what we do. It takes an enormous amount of work to achieve what may appear to be nothing at all. I remember someone once saying to me about *Friends*, "What's the big deal about the costumes? They just wear jeans in every scene." The truth is, there were nine costume changes per episode, and with six main actors that's fifty-four changes right there. Add three guest stars per show—each with six changes—and you're suddenly looking at seventy-two costume changes in a single half-hour sitcom. It's not just jeans!

Design for Dolly Parton's Country Music Hall of Fame dress. Illustration by Michelle Lucas

Working with Producers
When producers, studios and networks have the final say

Can you talk about the relationship between the costume designer and producers?

When a producer has seen what we can do—how we manage to create something
visually exciting while staying on budget—they often become our greatest advocates.
A good relationship built on trust and results means they are likely to recommend me
and my team to directors on future projects. That kind of continuity makes everything
run more smoothly because there's already mutual respect and a shared shorthand in
place.

For producers, especially when large budgets are involved, hiring the costume
designer and supervisor is a major decision. We're people they'll be working closely
with every day, and if things don't go well, the impact on the production can be significant. I've been lucky to have strong, long-term relationships with many producers
that have been built on trust and creative alignment from the very beginning of my
career. Early on, I worked with George Perkins on maybe ten or eleven Movies of the
Week—that partnership really launched my career in costume design. Later, I collaborated with major producers like Kevin Bright, Marta Kauffman, and David Crane, as
well as Judd Apatow.

Joe

The costume department's relationship with the producers can be tricky. The
designer has created a look and identified specific garments, the actors are
comfortable with their costumes, and the director has signed off on everything, but
the producer might have something completely different in mind. That's where the
costume department needs to be able to speak up firmly in support of the actor's
comfort and the design aesthetic of the show, and be able to persuasively explain
why something that is being presented is a good and conscious choice. A lot of
times, I feel like producers think that because they are so good at choosing their
own clothes, they must be good at choosing a character's costume. That can be
challenging.

Ideally we have built a relationship with the producers which makes them supportive of our choices. The key component in building that kind of relationship is communication. What we want to avoid is a situation where people are giving ultimatums—"It's this or nothing"—because this is a visual and collaborative business where we all need to work together to get to a place where actors feel comfortable and where the clothes they are wearing help them convey the character they're portraying.

Gavin

There are many kinds of producers on a project, and their involvement depends on the production and their specific role. Some are hands-on creatively, collaborating closely with the director and department heads, while others represent the financial or executive interests of a studio, network, or production company. Because producers ultimately control the budget, the costume department often works with them to get approval on major purchases or to negotiate the number of crew days needed to execute a particular creative vision. Their focus might range from managing costs to ensuring the final product aligns with the larger goals of the production.

In film, the director typically defines the creative vision for the entire shoot, and producers tend to play a more supervisory or supportive role—though they may still attend key prep meetings where character and costume choices are discussed. In TV, however, the dynamic is often different. Because episodic series rotate directors, it's the showrunners and producers who maintain the overall look, tone, and continuity of the show. In those cases, the costume department often works more directly with producers to ensure that wardrobe decisions stay consistent with the established visual world of the series, even as different directors come and go. Ultimately, our goal is to execute the costume designer's vision while staying aligned with the creative leadership that guides the project—whether that comes from the director, the showrunner, or the producers.

What's the difference between working with a producer on a film and producers on a series?

On a film, there are levels of producers. Line producers hire the crew, monitor the shooting, and are on set every day. They control the day-to-day production and are responsible for keeping the production on schedule and on budget. Executive producers can be responsible for financing the production, or they may work for the studios. Sometimes the writers, or even the actors, can be executive producers. Like wardrobe, producers have their own hierarchy, but in film most of the creative decisions about costume are going to be made by the director. In TV the producers typically stay with the production for the whole run of the series while the directors usually change from episode to episode, which means that producers often have more creative control than the director. As a result, on TV I frequently need to get the producers involved in decisions about the costumes I want to use. A TV director could be micromanaged by the producers and by production, whereas on film, the director usually has the final say on anything creative.

Does the costume designer have dealings with the studio executives?

Early on, when our costume ideas are initially being approved, the studio is usually involved. As the production progresses, especially in films, once they feel comfortable with what the producers, the director, and the costume designer are planning, the studio will step back. But on TV they usually stay involved throughout the run of the show. On TV shows I've even had the head of the studio come up and talk to me about costumes, particularly if there is something they aren't happy with, something they want us to rethink. That never happens on a film.

Designs of costumes for Ashton Kutcher and Brittany Murphy in *Just Married* (2003).
Illustration by Angela Carper.

Working with Other Departments

To tell the story successfully, there must be communication and collaboration

Can you talk about the interaction between the costume department and other departments in the production?

Collaboration is so important. A costume never exists in isolation; it's part of a larger visual and emotional narrative shaped by lighting, set design, and the director's vision. Each department has its own priorities and pressures, yet the success of the project depends on our ability to integrate those individual efforts into a single, cohesive vision. What the audience experiences when watching a film or TV show is the result of all of us working together.

Collaboration begins early, in both one-on-one meetings with the director or showrunner and in larger gatherings of all department heads. It's in those conversations that we align our visions and identify potential challenges. On many productions, the proximity of departments helps, too. My team is often located right next to production design and props, so we see each other daily. That constant interaction allows us to troubleshoot, brainstorm, and make sure we're all visually supporting the same story.

The creative synergy on *Friends* was extraordinary. Production designers John Shaffner and Joe Stewart, along with set decorator Greg Grande, were instrumental in defining the show's iconic aesthetic. Even though each of us worked within our own discipline, we were always in sync—constantly problem-solving and refining details together. Despite the record-breaking pace of that show, it remained one of the most harmonious and creatively unified productions I've ever been part of.

Of course, not every project works that way. When communication or collaboration breaks down between departments, the results can be chaotic—and possibly disastrous for production as well as the final product. One time we were preparing for a funeral scene set in the '50s, the very first scene shooting on day one of production. My team had spent weeks putting together racks of authentic, mostly black garments from the period, and I arrived on set that morning filled with the usual excitement that comes after so much preparation. But when I went to check on the background actors, what immediately caught my attention were the hairstyles, which were completely wrong for the period. The shapes, the finishes—everything felt off. The hats we had planned for the scene didn't even fit properly because of the way people's hair had been styled. When the principal actors arrived, the problem was even more obvious. The wigs were poorly cut and didn't resemble anything close to the era we were trying to evoke. One of the male actors had even altered his hairline in a way that made it impossible to achieve the right look. It was a perfect and very unfortunate example of how easily a lack of communication between departments can derail the visual integrity of a scene. Getting the right look on camera is never just about the costumes—it depends on constant collaboration among costume, hair, makeup, props, production design, even camera and lighting. When those departments aren't in sync, the audience feels it. Coordination and mutual understanding are essential to making the world of a film believable.

How do you make sure that the costumes fit in with the rest of the visual elements in a scene?

That's something we discuss very early on with the director and the camera team, usually in the first production meetings as we go through the script scene by scene. The goal is always visual cohesion. We talk about tone, palette, and how each scene will be lit and framed. If a character needs to stand out, we'll strategize how to achieve that through color, silhouette, texture, or even the way the shot is composed, while keeping everything harmonious within the larger visual world of the film.

A good example is from an Indian wedding sequence I designed where the bride was meant to wear red—the traditional color for South Indian brides. My first instinct was to put the groom in white, which would have felt clean and celebratory next to her. But the director said, "I don't want him in white. He's a big guy—it'll make him look larger." I suggested lavender instead. Lavender and red are a beautiful combination—authentic to the culture, elegant, and visually dynamic. It also created the right balance between the two leads while setting them apart from the rest of the crowd. Once that was decided, I reached out to the production designer because I wanted to make sure our costume palette wouldn't clash with his decor. His presentation for the wedding set was nearly finalized, so he sent it over. I asked him to pull back on the reds in the areas behind the bride so she wouldn't visually disappear. Instead, I suggested soft pastels and creams for the background, which would allow her red dress to "pop" on camera. We later had a Zoom meeting with the director, production designer, DP, producers, and actors to walk everyone through the look and feel of the scene. These kinds of discussions are critical early in the process—not only to ensure that all departments are aligned creatively but also to give us enough time to build or source the costumes properly.

Adam Sandler and Jennifer Aniston in their white costumes on set video monitor
in the Indian wedding scene, *Murder Mystery 2* (2022).

I had worked on Indian wedding scenes before, including *Murder Mystery 2*,
where I had to costume a room full of five hundred extras in traditional attire—an
explosion of color. In a scene like that, if the leads are in bright colors, they'll get lost
in the frame, so I dressed Adam Sandler and Jennifer Aniston in white, ensuring the
audience's eye would always find them.

To plan that scene, I created a color collage by cutting out paper swatches in
all the hues of the guest costumes and arranging them to represent the frame. Then I
placed two small white dots for the leads. It became a visual map that I could share
with the director and production designer so we could see how the colors would play
together on screen. A simple, low-tech approach, but it made everything crystal clear
for everyone involved.

*Can you talk about the relationship between the costume department and the assistant
directors?*

Joe
We almost always shoot out of sequence, skipping around back and forth in the
script storyline on different shooting days. The AD department creates the shooting
schedule and changes it almost daily during the shoot. I always work closely with

the first assistant director on scheduling so I know how and when my garments will be moving and the volume and exact nature of the staff I will need to accomplish that. For me this is a crucial relationship which helps me to accurately figure out the timing of both cast members on camera during the shoot, as well as arranging for cast members to travel in ahead of time for fittings. The ADs coordinate the timeline of everything just outside of what the lens is seeing as well as what needs to be in front of the camera on any given day.

Gavin

The ADs run the entire set. They aren't making creative or style decisions but they do make sure everyone is in the right place at the right time. The ADs handle the daily call sheets, shooting schedules, and might be the first line of communication with the director depending on the project. If we have a question about a scene or costume continuity, we might go through them rather than interrupt the shoot. Their job is to manage the flow of production, and ours is to stay on their schedule so costumes never become the reason filming slows down. They also manage the background actors. The ADs bring them to us for dressing, then take them to set and place them in the scene. We'll have a costumer there to make sure each background performer looks right—for example, making sure no one stands too close to a principal actor in a similar color or pattern. We're helping "paint the picture," and that collaboration only works when there's mutual understanding with the ADs.

The ADs also coordinate the turnover between scenes for principal actors, which involves wardrobe, hair, makeup, and sound. We're all communicating about the actors' timeline: when they are traveling to and from set and when they are expected to be camera-ready, whether that means changing their clothes, prepping for a stunt or action scene, or rewiring their mic, without holding up production.

In the end, it's about staying one step ahead. A good working rhythm with the ADs keeps the shoot running smoothly and gives the director as much time as possible to focus on the work.

Can you talk about the relationship between costumers and the sound department?

Gavin

We work very closely with the sound department—much more than most people realize. When an actor arrives on set, one of the first things that needs to happen is getting them wired for sound. That means the sound team has to place a hidden microphone and battery pack somewhere on the actor's body or inside their clothing. Because costumers understand how the garments fit,

With Bud Cort on the set of *Die Laughing* (1980). I didn't design the film, but was hired to design and create his 18k gold and cloisonné cheek pin.

move, and what the camera will see, we collaborate with sound to find a placement that's both invisible on camera and comfortable for the actor. Sometimes this means sewing a mic pack into the interior of a costume piece—even inside underwear or the lining of a jacket—so it stays secure and hidden. If sound can't place a wire on the costume, they'll be forced to use a boom mic instead. We're constantly troubleshooting with sound to make sure they get the best possible sound quality without compromising the look or integrity of the costume.

Helen Mirren in *Phil Spector* (2011). Photograph by Phillip Caruso.

Navigating Challenges During Production
Costume changes on the fly are very much a part of our job

Have you ever had to redesign a character's wardrobe in the middle of a production?

It has happened many times in my thirty-six-year career, but one instance that stands out was in David Mamet's film *Phil Spector*. Al Pacino was playing the record producer Phil Spector, on trial for murder in the film. His co-star, playing his lawyer, was originally Bette Midler. I met with Linda Keeney Baden, Spector's actual criminal defense lawyer in the murder trial, in her New York apartment, and mentally noted all the personal details. There were so many clues: her dyed blonde hair, large jewelry, and Jersey girl vibe. I then fit Bette at her home. We were very close to commencing principal photography but at the very last minute, Bette's back went out and she was unable to do the film. The role had to be re-cast and in an instant Helen Mirren was hired to replace her. Lucky for me she was a dream to work with and completely open to my direction. Together we shaped who this woman was—her authority, her vulnerability—all through what she wore. I watched Helen discover the character of Linda through the clothing. It's a good example of how re-casting can send the entire costume design on a different trajectory—in this case, a deeply inspiring one.

Can you talk about the clearance issues costume designers face?

Company names, logos, images, works of art, things like that are intellectual property. They all belong to someone, a company or people, and no one else can use them without the owner's permission. In order to include clothing in a film or episode that has, for example, a logo or person's face on it, the production needs to get permission, a license, to use it in the film. We keep this in mind when we choose clothing, but there are people at the studios, networks and production companies that specialize in clearing the rights to all of this. When we were doing *Freaks and Geeks*, most of James Franco's wardrobe was sourced from vintage stores and LA costume houses. We put him in a perfectly aged vintage t-shirt with a trucking company logo on it. Everyone loved it. The producers had people responsible for clearances, but somehow this t-shirt slipped through the cracks. We found out much later that the trucking company was still in business and they ended up suing the studio for a substantial amount of money for using their logo without their permission. Because of claims like this, over the course of my career, clearance procedures have become stricter, and it's gotten to the point where I am now extremely aware of anything on clothing that might create a legal problem. Nowadays it's standard that when we need a graphic on a piece of clothing, we have to design the graphic ourselves and put it on new clothes that we distress to look vintage. This avoids all clearance issues entirely.

Joe

Often clearance becomes a game of whether the studio or the producers want to give away free advertising. If a character is wearing a hat with a Coca-Cola logo, do they want to give free promotion to Coca-Cola or not? If the character is wearing a band's t-shirt, we would have to deal with the band so we can use their name and/or logo and get the person who made the artwork for the band to sign off as well. Sometimes the owner of the name, artwork or logo, doesn't want their work on the t-shirt worn by a certain character because this could affect how the public perceives their brand. As soon as a garment or accessory with a specific name or brand is included in the script, a different level of clearance is required, one that usually involves experts working for the producers or the studio.

What challenges have you faced working in extreme environments?

Weather is always a challenge. On *Dig*, we had a scene with two dozen male extras dressed as Orthodox Jews in long black coats and black hats. The coats were made of lightweight fabric and we were shooting in freezing temperatures. This created a very difficult situation for the costumers, the director and especially those background actors. We used warming jackets between takes, but it was rough for us as well as the actors. I've also worked in extreme heat, like in Mexico and Hawaii, or unexpectedly warm conditions, like when we shot on a very hot day in Budapest and had dressed everyone in wool coats. Keeping people hydrated and safe is always the priority, and, where the conditions warrant, we send out notices reminding background cast and other cast to bring coats and cold weather gear with them to the set. We sometimes end up dressing directors head-to-toe in warm gear to keep them comfortable when we are out shooting in a very cold location. More often it's the hot locations that create the most problems.

What happens if there is a need to do additional shooting weeks or months after the principal photography has finished and your department has already wrapped?

As the designer, I'm not usually involved once a film has wrapped, although if it's a huge film with a lot of moving parts I may ask production to keep me on through wrap. If there are going to be reshoots—some added scenes or existing scenes that need to be shot again for some reason—I need to know because as the designer, I am ultimately the one responsible. In recent years I've left the wrap to Gavin and Joe. It would obviously be a nightmare if the producer or director wanted to do reshoots only to find that they didn't have the costumes they needed.

Joe

The wrap is very important. Once we walk away from a production, we bag every costume and tag it with descriptions, and put it into grouped bags based on the character and what scenes this outfit was worn in, along with detailed notes about garment sizing and everything you could imagine having to do with it. Who manufactured each individual garment? What size was the actor wearing? What alterations were made to it? Then it gets saved and stored until the film is released.

Films are often in the editing phase or being screened for a test audience when filmmakers realize they need an insert shot of a character or even have to shoot additional scenes. They have to get back into those bags quickly and efficiently because when any kind of a reshoot takes place, it will usually be with a much smaller skeleton crew that is working on a tight budget. If cast members have gained or lost weight since the original shoot, there may have to be alterations to the garment. If it's an independent production, they will often only store principal garments and sell everything else. If it's a studio production, initially everything gets stored at a storage facility based at the studio, but eventually anything not worn by a principal actor gets released into the studio's stock department and used on another show that needs similar garments. Items that were worn by stars are typically archived and sometimes will be used to promote the film during press junkets or travel to special screenings like premieres or even a ten-year anniversary. The days of just having a garage sale in the wardrobe truck don't really exist anymore, at least on the larger scale projects that I work on, because every item may be needed at a moment's notice in the not-too-distant future.

Once the shooting has started and actors are spending long days wearing their costumes, can you talk about what it takes to keep the clothes clean and ready for the next shooting day?

Joe

We need to maintain the clothing so it's usable throughout the production, which is a big job. We use cleaning products that are gentle on the garments because, believe it or not, during the production you can actually start to see the color of

Olivia Wilde adorned in accessories in *Year One* (2009).

a pair of jeans change due to the daily washings if you're using detergents with heavy chemicals or cleaning power. Sometimes, despite our efforts, daily cleaning takes a toll, which is why we try to have more than one of everything so we can rotate them through the production, allowing them to fade gradually and at the same pace. What you don't want is a shirt to be bright lavender one day and dull lavender the next, which is why we try to do some aging or cleaning before anything goes on camera. There are always last-minute changes, additional wardrobe we didn't prepare in advance. Those garments we must be extremely careful with. We need to age them very gently as the production goes on, making sure there is no sudden shift in color.

Gavin

The location of the shoot, the size of the budget, and the value or fabric content of the garment all play the biggest roles in how we maintain costumes. Plenty of locations don't have cleaning services that can turn around dry cleaning or laundering in 24 hours. In cities like New York or LA, we're lucky— you can finish shooting late at night, send out the costumes, and have them back the next morning cleaned, pressed, and camera-ready. But on location, where that kind of service might not exist, costumers have to be much more judicious about how we care for garments. At the end of the day, we have to decide which pieces really need washing. Does the actor wear it again tomorrow? Do we have multiples? What are the chances the fabric will shrink or the color will fade if we wash it? If something goes wrong during cleaning, we could find ourselves in a tough spot the following shoot day.

In those cases, the set and truck costumers often end up treating and laundering the clothes ourselves. We usually have a washer and dryer either on the wardrobe truck or in the office and use different techniques depending on the fabric, dirt, or damage. Smaller items like socks and underwear are easy— we have multiples and can swap them out daily. But where we don't have that flexibility, we'll treat items with alcohol spray to keep them fresh and odor-free for the next use.

For vintage or delicate garments, we handle them with extra care, sometimes spot-cleaning by hand or using gentle steaming methods to preserve their texture and integrity. Of course, all this ties back to continuity—making sure the costume looks the same from one shooting day to the next, no matter how many times it's been worn, cleaned, or repaired.

Me and Dolly Parton, wearing a costume I designed for *Heavens to Betsy*, 1995.

Memorable Projects, Memorable Challenges
Behind-the-scenes stories from key productions in my career

Can you tell us about the films, series and plays you have costume designed?

In nearly forty years as a costume designer, I've designed 44 films—not counting 21 movies of the week; maybe a thousand episodes of 41 TV series and more than 80 pilots; a handful of commercials and shorts; and for the theater, two musicals and a period drama. The highlights would probably be the work I did with Bright, Kaufman and Crane; Judd Apatow and his collaborators; David Mamet; and most recently with John Francis Daley and Jonathan Goldstein, as well as my work for Dolly Parton.

How did you come to work on Friends?

I first met Marta Kauffman, David Crane, and Kevin Bright when I interviewed for their show *Family Album*, which starred Peter Scolari, Pamela Reed, and a very young Giovanni Ribisi. I wanted to make a good impression, so I borrowed a suit from my friend Alice—an olive-green Versace number with a very short miniskirt and a double-breasted jacket with big shoulders. I paired it with brown opaque tights and chunky brown-olive heels. The interview went perfectly. I got the job, and as I was leaving, Marta looked at me and said, "Just make sure all the girls on the show look as good as you do." The moment I stepped outside, I burst out laughing. If only she'd known I had borrowed everything I was wearing!

 Family Album turned out to be a bit of a wild ride—they even recast one of the lead actors the day before shooting began—but that show began my creative relationship with Marta, David, and Kevin. Not long after, Marta told me about a new project they were developing called *Friends*. She and David had written the pilot back in college and recently pulled it out of a drawer. I had just given birth to my daughter, Lily, when I got a call from Marta while I was still in the hospital. It was a Thursday, and she said she wanted me to start on *Friends* that coming Monday. As soon as I got home from the hospital, I started interviewing crew members at my house on the weekend—my newborn daughter Lily lying in a basket right next to my desk. I did the pilot and stayed on for all ten seasons of *Friends*. The pilot was unlike anything I'd worked on before. The premise was fresh, and the cast—Courteney Cox, Jennifer Aniston, Lisa Kudrow, Matt LeBlanc, Matthew Perry, and David Schwimmer—had undeniable chemistry. What struck me most was how the show's simplicity and relatability resonated even in the early days. The costumes needed to reflect the authenticity of their characters—effortless, cool, and timeless, but with distinct personalities that would make each character stand out.

The only thing I knew about network TV at the time was that the clothes were terrible. I would run through the channels and shriek that the styles and colors hurt my eyes. It was bad denim and more denim. Oversized and awkward. Everyone looked uncomfortable. The '90s were a challenge, too—everything was boxy and shapeless. I was determined that *Friends* would be different.

As a painter, I had always seen the world through color, form, and light. The screen, I realized, was no different from a canvas—it was another two-dimensional surface waiting to be composed. Instead of focusing solely on clothing, I began by thinking about the entire frame: the background, the furniture, the props, the way the actors existed in space. The clothes weren't just costumes; they were part of a larger visual assemblage. With every scene, I wasn't just dressing characters—I was creating a painting.

Initially, Marta envisioned the characters in jeans—comfortable, casual, easy. But I pushed back. I wanted to create something visually distinct, something aspirational yet familiar. She trusted me, and I began assigning each character a palette, a texture, a visual identity. In the ten-year evolution of the show, those palettes expanded and styles shifted as the characters grew and their lives changed, just like in real life. Hairstyles evolved, too. They matured, and their clothing often became more sophisticated. Every choice was intentional, every detail carefully considered. It wasn't just about fashion—it was about world-building, storytelling through color and texture.

This is how I began:

Monica—black, white, gray, with accents of red and burgundy.

Rachel—blues and greens, always rich in texture.

Phoebe—bohemian layers, flowing fabrics, eclectic patterns and accessories.

Ross—professorial in tweeds and corduroys, plaid shirts layered over t-shirts, classic khakis.

Chandler—vintage-inspired shirts, blazers, quirky ties, Hush Puppies.

Joey—flannels and chenille sweaters, and—most importantly—a perfectly worn-in leather jacket. Ironically, that "struggling actor" jacket started out as an Armani. We aged and distressed it until it looked like he'd owned it for years.

Each week, for every episode, I would create a board—a visual roadmap for the show's costumes. I assembled Polaroid photos of wardrobe options and studied how they interacted within a scene. Most scenes involved multiple actors—if not all six—

Drawings of original costumes for the lead characters in *Friends* (1994).
Illustration by Lois DeArmand.

sometimes including guest cast. The sheer volume of costume changes was staggering. Between changes for the lead actors and guest stars, we typically had more than eighty wardrobe changes for cast and guest cast, all for a single half-hour sitcom.

The schedule was relentless. We'd receive the script on Monday for the table read and by Thursday we were already doing pre-shoots, leading into the full shoot on Friday. That left only part of Tuesday and Wednesday for fittings—and let's face it, the cast hated fittings. Some more than others.

Fitting sessions, though, could be unexpectedly revealing. One of my favorite memories involves Jennifer, who from the very beginning had a wonderful instinct for what looked right on her and what suited Rachel's evolving personality. Sometimes, when we'd have multiple racks prepped for fittings, she'd spot a piece that had been pulled for another character and say, "That feels like Rachel." She was often absolutely right. It became a kind of unspoken collaboration between us—her intuition and my vision working in sync. Jennifer had such a natural sense of Rachel's style and helped define it in ways that made the character iconic. It was a perfect reminder that costume design, at its best, is a dialogue—between designer, actor, and character—and that chemistry is what makes something truly timeless.

Did you make many of the costumes for Friends *in-house?*

My original idea was to design and make all the costumes in-house, but that plan didn't last long. To create clothing properly, you must have multiple opportunities for fittings with each of the actors, and on *Friends* the shooting schedule simply didn't allow for that. I managed to squeeze in one fitting a week and could design a few pieces whenever possible: shirts for Chandler, a dress or suit here and there, Rachel's coffee shop aprons, and, of course, all the "gag" costumes. But to make costumes you must have the time to do fittings.

The writers—who became our friends—believed they were doing us a favor by turning clothing gags into a major part of the show. After the first season, we begged them to ease up. There were the holiday episodes—Halloween, Christmas, Thanksgiving—and then the wild ones, like the Thanksgiving episode spanning seven time periods where Phoebe, as a Civil War nurse, gets her arm blown off!

Since you didn't have the chance to make the clothes yourself, where did you get the signature look for the show—clothes that weren't oversized and not all denim?

When I designed the film *S.F.W.,* I met Pamela Skaist, who, along with her partner Gela Nash-Taylor, had a clothing line that specialized in maternity clothes. She was the wife of our director. When *Friends* started in 1994, I was aching for different kinds of "cool" clothing—pieces that showed the body in a way that was effortless but intentional. Pam and Gela would send me things, including the tiny t-shirts I had been

Drawings of various *Friends* costumes (1994).
Illustration by Maggie P.

searching for. Rachel rocked them, and those tees were already impacting what real people were wearing. It was the beginning of a new wave.

Then, in 1997, Pam and Gela rebranded their company as Juicy Couture and suddenly the whole landscape changed. LA—and soon, the world—embraced this fresh take on casual luxury. The velour tracksuits, the fitted tanks, the playful, sexy ease of it all. It was everything I had been moving toward, and it aligned perfectly with what I wanted for the show. This wasn't just about Rachel's look—it influenced the guys, too. Gone were the baggy silhouettes of the early '90s. Instead, the *Friends* wardrobe became a reflection of what people wanted to wear in real life. It was polished, sexy, and just the right amount of effortless.

Looking back, it's clear—this wasn't just a styling decision. It was a shift, a moment where TV fashion and real-life trends met, shaping each other in ways no one could have predicted. And it all started with a search for something different.

Given the speed that the series was being shot, how did you keep track of everything?

In addition to the boards, I also created massive charts that mapped out every scene. They were meticulously color-coded to track what each character was wearing. These charts were our bible—guiding us through the entire process of building the show. On performance nights, we'd create miniature versions for each actor, posting them on their dressing room doors. This way, they could visually track their changes, knowing exactly when and what they would be wearing.

My biggest nightmare? An actor approaching me at the last minute and saying, "Can I wear this instead?" In such cases, I take a deep breath and calmly explain, "Actually, someone else is wearing that color, so it would be best if you stuck with what we've set…" Often, their response is, "But in real life, people wear the same colors!" This is true, and had it been discussed prior to shooting I may have been persuaded, but in the stress of the moment, it usually isn't possible.

Can you think of some examples of this work that is now considered "iconic"?

Today almost everything about *Friends* is considered iconic, but in the beginning— when it was first presented to me—it was simply about six characters. Six distinct individuals, each with a specific personality, yet defined by being part of this tight-knit group of friends.

As I met the actors, I began to imagine who these people were and where they were headed in life. What they wore would play a huge part in telling their stories and shaping their identities. Jennifer's character, Rachel, for instance, was the "rich girl." How do we convey that visually? How do we make her stand apart from Monica or Phoebe? It wasn't just about labels or price tags—it was about the *look*: the silhouette, the texture, the palette, the subtle suggestion of privilege. I broke down each character into their own unique color and texture world.

At the same time, their clothes had to work harmoniously together, since the six of them so often shared the frame. Most of the scenes took place in "the loft"—that lavender-hued apartment filled with eclectic tchotchkes—so the costumes also needed to live comfortably within that environment.

TV moves fast. We didn't have the luxury of meeting weekly with the set decorator or production designer, but we were all instinctively on the same wavelength. From the pilot on, we established a look that carried through ten seasons—one that evolved naturally as the characters' lives did. As their careers and incomes grew, their wardrobes subtly reflected that evolution: the fabrics got finer, the fits more refined, the choices more confident. You could *see* their lives changing.

Left and following page: Collage of fitting Polaroids of the main characters from the pilot and season 1 of *Friends* (1994).

Set photographers: Joey Del Valle (1994-95), Ron P. Jaffe (2000-2004).

Top: Phoebe as a Civil War nurse (1998).

Botton: Ross and Chandler dressed in '80s costumes in the style of *Miami Vice* (1998).

Top: Rachel dressed as a bridesmaid (1996).

Bottom: Rachel dressed in knee socks and plaid skirt (1995).

But *Friends* wasn't about realism. It was an elevated version of reality—an aspirational lifestyle, slightly idealized, where everything from the furniture to the paint on the walls and the clothes created a heightened, dreamlike version of everyday life. The wardrobe was as much a part of that storytelling as any line of dialogue. Now, more than three decades later, people are still fascinated by what the characters wore. I think that's partly because I wasn't chasing trends. I wasn't trying to mirror what was popular at the time; I wanted to create looks that felt original—perhaps even slightly ahead of their time. Clothes that were elevated, interesting, and reflected my own idealized version of what that generation's fashion *could* be.

Was any of the Friends *costuming later produced or sold commercially?*

At the beginning of season two, I talked to the president of Warner Bros. TV about merchandising. The discussions continued for a couple of years, but by the time Warner Bros. was ready to move forward, the actors had gotten so famous it was of no interest to them. In the early years when they were less sophisticated, we probably could have done something, but as they got more savvy and the show became so wildly successful, there was no way that they were going to allow anyone to sell clothes with their likeness on the hang tags. Fans clamored for the clothing we featured on the show, and decades later the emails still come in droves. People of all ages from around the world write to me as they discover the show for the first time.

Because of the success of *Friends*, in 2001 I made a deal to design a Debra McGuire clothing collection at the exclusive Henri Bendel department store in New York. I was also approached at that time about designing a line of clothing for the Home Shopping Network. I designed affordable pieces of fashion-forward clothing in our New York studio and manufactured them in Hong Kong. I hosted the show for three years until the routine of flying to Florida to the HSN Studios, to introduce the clothes to customers in the TV audience, got to be too much for me. This experience led to the offer of designing and selling clothes on Home Shopping Europe, a European network in Munich, where my English was dubbed into German. I left after a year because it was too much time and effort to travel this distance, while juggling everything else. Then, from 1995 to 2005, in addition to my costume design work, I had an atelier in Los Angeles, where I created seasonal, in-house ready-to-wear and couture collections. Many of these outfits were purchased specifically to be worn for film or TV industry events.

How did Freaks and Geeks *happen?*

I had already met Jake Kasdan, the director of the pilot, and Judd Apatow, the producer. They called me to interview and I was fortunate enough to land the job. I remember

Debra in front of her clothing store in Pacific Palisades, circa 1995.

Fitting Lisa Kudrow in her real-life wedding dress that I designed in 1995.

thinking at the time that they most likely hired me to get the latest *Friends* updates, even though they acted like they could care less. *Friends* and Jennifer were the talk of the town and on the cover of every magazine.

It was great working on *Freaks and Geeks*, which had such a different energy than *Friends* and the other Bright Kaufman Crane TV shows I designed. I would walk off the set of *Veronica's Closet*, which was often a problematic shoot for me, and come on to the set of *Freaks and Geeks*. The kids there—everyone was so young—would all greet me with kisses and hugs. It became my happy place. The contrast between shows was dramatic.

How did you begin your costuming for Freaks and Geeks?

It was a period teen drama series set in 1980 in a suburban high school in Michigan. The show tackled social issues through an authentic, deeply human lens. Judd and Paul Feig were the creators and showrunners.

Paul had created a "bible" for each department, detailing everything from character backstories to the textures and context of their world. I had never seen anything like it. With so much clearly laid out, my job was much easier—no second-guessing, no designing in the dark. It was my role as a costume designer to bring the creator's vision to life, and this resource made it feel like I had a direct line into Paul's mind. It was thrilling.

I'll never forget the first production meeting. Jake, the director, sat at the head of the table, surrounded by seasoned crew members. He was maybe 22 years old, but his command of the room and his maturity was clear for everyone to see. He spoke about working with young actors and how important it was for us, the crew, to be role models—mindful of our language, behavior, and energy on set.

Meeting the cast for their first fittings was equally unforgettable. Linda Cardellini arrived with a friend from Loyola University, giggling and full of excitement. As we tried on clothes, we talked non-stop—they loved the period styles. Even though the show was set in 1980, I skewed the wardrobe slightly earlier, into the late '70s. Growing up in Ohio, I knew firsthand that Midwestern fashion always lagged behind what my friends were wearing in New York and California. That kind of detail—and all the small, lived-in authenticity—was what made *Freaks and Geeks* special.

Lindsay's army jacket was just one of the many vintage pieces I pulled for *Freaks and Geeks*. Nothing was branded—everything was secondhand, thrifted, or sourced to feel as authentic as possible to the era. Today, the grunge and vintage styles from the show are perfectly on trend. I remember standing in front of a rack of vintage clothes for the fitting, shaking my head and thinking, "These are not the most attractive clothes." Years later, Heather Snowden of *Highsnobiety* interviewed me about the show's costumes and that jacket.

"It's [an] identity piece for all young people who have some sense of rebellion. I think that's really powerful, and every character had that," McGuire says. "It was a very conscious thing in creating these characters to be sort of the essence of what they represent socially and politically." Put another way, each character's outfit is a uniform based on "who they are in the hierarchy and scene."

Take Lindsay's Vietnam War-era military jacket, for example. "It's such an interesting piece because she straddled both worlds," McGuire says, referencing the character's affiliation to both a freak scene forever chain-smoking outside the cafeteria and her studies. "She's a good girl, she's a smart girl, and yet she has that sense of rebellion and being attracted to people who are musical, who are in another realm. That army jacket is a place for her to hide behind and identify with, and it becomes a really important piece."

McGuire might have found "Midwest style" synonymous with "lack of style," but the cast felt pretty differently about her wardrobe choices. "Each actor would come into their fitting and go, 'Oh my God, I love this. I want it!'" she recalls. "And that's when you realize that there's so much about fashion and trends that is so psychological in terms of what you're used to seeing, what you've never seen, what looks fresh, and what looks new. These kids had never seen clothes that looked like this before."

Shortly after James Franco received his script, he called me wanting to discuss his character and really dig into who this guy was. He told me he was planning to fly to Paul Feig's hometown, just to walk around, get a sense of the place, and maybe pick up a few pieces of clothing. This was a first for me, especially coming from an actor so young. Over the next few days, he called me three or four more times, all about wardrobe. I couldn't believe his intensity and curiosity, and I looked forward to meeting him. I remember the day he walked into my office, this scruffy young guy, disheveled in jeans and a t-shirt, his hair messy and a little dirty. Under his arm, he carried a book—*The Stranger* by Albert Camus—and a backpack with a few pieces of clothing. I rolled my eyes at Joe Mastrolia, as if to say, "This should be interesting."

At first, I thought he was just a kid trying to be an intellectual. But as we talked, I realized I couldn't have been more wrong. He grew up in Palo Alto, the son of Stanford professors. As I said earlier, I was shocked to learn that his grandmother owned the Japanese art gallery in Cleveland that I loved to visit when I was a kid. The more we spoke, the more he channeled James Dean, and when he left, I turned to Joe and said, "He's got that *Rebel Without a Cause* energy." Years later, when he played James Dean, I wasn't the least bit surprised. Since Franco's character, Daniel Desario, was the pot-smoking bad boy of the show, his wardrobe needed to reflect that. James's wardrobe was sourced from vintage stores and LA costume houses. When we put him in aged vintage t-shirts and jeans, he very much looked the part of the rebel. His aged green leather jacket became iconic.

How did you envision the overall look of the costumes on Freaks and Geeks?

Designing the pilot for that show was a masterclass in detail. Every element of the characters' costumes was considered, discussed, torn apart and put back together. Jake and the creative team were present for most of the initial fittings. For me, the challenge wasn't just about recreating 1980—it was about making the world feel real, lived-in, and timeless. I didn't want *Freaks and Geeks* to look like a typical period piece where every element screamed a specific era. Instead, the goal was to create something that felt natural, as if we had stepped into these characters' lives rather than dressed them up for nostalgia's sake.

To achieve this, I decided we would over-dye all of the clothing in a subtle gray or brown tone, muting the hues, values, and saturation of every color. This technique softened the overall palette, ensuring that nothing felt too crisp, too new, or too artificially retro. It allowed the wardrobe to blend seamlessly with the cinematography and production design, giving the show its signature, almost documentary-like realism. The result was more than just a visual choice—it became part of the show's identity, a quiet but powerful tool that made *Freaks and Geeks* feel like a memory unfolding rather than a recreation of the past. Working with Judd and Jake taught me so much. Comedy is already heightened, so costumes need to stay rooted to support the humor without tipping into parody. For the costumes to support the comedy, our efforts had to be subtle.

What looks were you going for with the different characters?

Take the first fitting we did with Martin Starr, who played Bill Haverchuck. He was about 16 or 17 at the time, and like so many of the young actors, he was a discovery. But we weren't quite sure what to make of him. The fitting took place at Universal Studios, and from the very first outfit, something unusual happened. Martin took the clothing we gave him and disappeared into the dressing room. He stayed there for what felt like an eternity. Then, maybe twenty minutes later, he finally emerged. This happened for every single outfit—and there were at least thirty for him to try on.

Jake and the creative team were there with me and my team, all of us waiting in the hallway for Martin to emerge from the dressing room. None of us knew what to make of it. Was he shy? Was he methodically examining each look in the mirror? Was he just messing with us? Thirty years later, I still don't know, but in hindsight, this might have been the dressing version of that slow, deadpan delivery that became Martin's

Main cast, *Freaks and Geeks* (1999).

comedic trademark. And in the end, his signature look—oversized glasses and classic rugby shirts—came together almost effortlessly. Dressed that way, Martin became Bill. Samm Levine as Neal was the preppiest of the boys and his signature style became collared shirts and vests, sometimes argyle.

Seth Rogan was just a teenager, a funny kid with a dry sense of humor and a hearty laugh. He was always quick with a sarcastic remark that could break any tension on set. His character, Ken Miller, was a wise-cracking realist, a bit detached from the drama of the group but always ready with a cutting remark or an eye roll. His wardrobe reflected his laid-back and slightly rebellious personality—black t-shirts, well-worn jeans, flannel shirts, and long-sleeve baseball tees. His "freak" aesthetic was a perfect blend of grunge and casual cool.

Jason Segel was 19 when he played the drummer Nick Andopolis, Lindsay's love interest and an endearing dreamer with a passion for music. He had a lanky swagger, a natural sexiness that was both awkward and charming, which I tried to enhance with his signature wardrobe. He often wore sleeveless t-shirts that showed off his long arms and relaxed posture, paired with corduroy jeans and big belt buckles that added to his laid-back, almost rock-star-in-training vibe. His iconic fleece-lined denim jacket became a staple, often slung over his shoulder in a way that seemed effortless and cool. Ringer and striped t-shirts were a frequent choice, adding to his vintage-inspired, slightly disheveled look. When he was behind the drum kit, twirling his drumsticks, he typically sported a baseball-style t-shirt with music logos, reinforcing his musician image. His wardrobe played up the idea that Nick was a passionate artist—one with more enthusiasm than actual talent—who had a deep love for rock and roll.

Busy Phillips played Kim Kelly, the tough, rebellious freak caught in a volatile relationship with Daniel. Kim came from a chaotic and often difficult home life, which shaped both her attitude and her style. Her wardrobe was simple and effortlessly cool—t-shirts, sweaters, and well-worn jeans, always topped with her iconic multi-blue geometric jacket. A white puka shell choker around her neck was a subtle nod to the era's trends, while her blonde hair, parted sharply down the center, gave her a fierce and unfiltered look.

You worked on numerous projects with Judd Apatow.

Several TV shows and quite a few films, in various capacities—sometimes he was the director, sometimes the producer, and often both. Early on there was a pilot called *Sick in the Head* that never got picked up, and right after *Freaks and Geeks* came *Undeclared*, which was another extraordinary experience. That show carried forward the same creative energy and emotional honesty that made *Freaks and Geeks* so special, and it gave me the opportunity to work with several of the same actors and crew members who would go on to shape the next generation of comedy. I also went on to design costumes for several of Judd's now classic films: *Anchorman, The 40-Year-Old Virgin, Knocked Up, Superbad,* and others. Each of these projects had its own distinct visual world, but they were all rooted in that same blend of humor and heart that defines Judd's work.

What's remarkable is how many doors *Freaks and Geeks* opened. To date, I've designed costumes for two dozen projects that trace back in some way to that series—whether through Judd himself or through directors, producers, and even actors from that show who went on to create their own projects and later brought me on board. In many ways, *Freaks and Geeks* became the creative nucleus from which so much of my later work evolved.

What do you remember from your work on Orange County?

Orange County—one of the projects that came out of my *Freaks and Geeks* work—was a film directed by Jake Kasdan and starred Jack Black and Colin Hanks. In that film, Lily Tomlin plays an eccentric guidance counselor who mistakenly sends the wrong student's transcript to Stanford. I was a big fan of Lily's work, especially her comedy stage shows. She was meticulous in her character development, and in the weeks before filming we had several conversations about how she envisioned her role. She wasn't just playing a part—she was building a person from the inside out. I made sure the hair and makeup teams were included in this process, giving them her insights and contact information so they could prepare accordingly.

For her wardrobe, I had a strong vision for her character's look and spent weeks sourcing outfits, pulling dresses, even sketching a design I felt was perfect for her. Among racks of carefully selected clothes was the dress I had custom-made. On the day of her fitting, I had the room ready—three full racks of clothing, shoes arranged neatly underneath, and a table filled with handbags and jewelry. When Lily arrived, I asked her to go through the racks and select pieces that resonated with her. She took her time, moving thoughtfully from one rack to the next, commenting on what worked and what didn't. Then, finally, she pulled out a dress and said, "This one is perfect." It was the dress I designed for her. She tried it on, it fit flawlessly, and we were done.

Throughout filming, I saw how some departments struggled with Lily's process because they hadn't taken the time to listen. But I did. That experience reinforced something I would carry with me throughout my career: every actor has a unique way of stepping into their role, and as a costume designer my job isn't just to design/dress them but to help the actor find a way to fully inhabit their character.

Can you tell us about your work with Judd on Anchorman?

Drawings and fitting photo of costume worn by Lily Tomlin in *Orange County* (2002).
Illustration by Anna Wyckoff.

When I did *Friends*, I was able to utilize my skills as a painter. I treated the characters' wardrobes as brushstrokes on a living canvas. *Anchorman* allowed me to take that concept to an entirely new level. Here, I wasn't just considering individual costumes—I was designing an entire visual language for the film. Every color, every texture, every fabric choice was deliberate, shaping the world of '70s San Diego with a heightened, almost surreal sense of authenticity.

My '70s palette included burnt oranges, mustards, rich browns, and, of course, the deep, luxurious burgundy that became an iconic part of the film's aesthetic. This was a period of bold, unselfconscious style, where men dressed with swagger and women exuded effortless elegance. I worked tirelessly to ensure that every scene carried this energy, balancing historical accuracy with a heightened comedic sensibility.

For the principal cast, I curated and created costumes that felt both authentic and slightly amplified, leaning into the film's satirical tone. I worked closely with costume houses, sourcing original garments when possible, but when I couldn't find the perfect item, I designed it myself. Every detail mattered: lapel widths, fabric

Above: designs for the main cast costumes of Anchorman (2004). Illustration by Susan Zarate.
Below: Photograph by Gemma La Mana.

weights, the drape of a jacket, the precise shade of a necktie. And beyond the leads, the background players were equally important. Massive crowd scenes required meticulous coordination, ensuring that even the extras looked like they had stepped straight out of a vintage *Esquire* spread.

What do you remember from some of your other work with Judd?

In 2007, I worked with him on *Superbad*, a comedy starring a young Emma Stone, Jonah Hill, Michael Cera, and Seth Rogen. The key costume was Jonah Hill's outfit: the piped cowboy shirt and glen plaid pants, both of which were based on garments that originally belonged to Jonah's character's dad. I designed the original shirt. We had to produce more than a dozen multiples to accommodate all the stunts and damage from what Jonah had to do on set. I dressed Michael Cera in striped shirts, brown cords, and a sweatshirt and then aged everything to create the right lived-in look.

Designing graphics for t-shirts became a huge focus of our work on that film. We had T- shirts with original band graphics and, of course, Jonah's Richard Pryor t-shirt. This was the first of many Judd Apatow productions where t-shirts were front and center.

In 2007 I worked on *Knocked Up*. The lead actors—Seth Rogen and Katherine Heigl—were originally going to have a few dozen costume changes, but in the end they had nearly a hundred each. Throughout the shoot, Judd kept having new ideas for scenes and action and each new idea meant a cascade of adjustments—new costumes, altered designs, last-minute fittings. It was exhausting but exhilarating.

After that I designed *Walk Hard: The Dewey Cox Story*, produced by Judd and directed by Jake Kasdan. It's the story of the legendary musical career of the fictional Dewey Cox, played by John C. Reilly. With costumes from the '40s, '50s and '60s, finding the right period appropriate clothes was a real challenge. We spent entire days—six to eight hours at a time—pulling racks of clothing from costume houses. The sheer volume of wardrobe we needed was staggering. We scoured the country to find what we needed. Palace Costume and Western Costume in LA became our second homes, along with countless vintage stores. Once we had gathered everything, we assessed what we needed to construct. Our workroom was busy nonstop producing stunning new period garments and reworking existing pieces. Background fittings were endless but precise. After the initial test screenings, we returned to shoot twelve additional scenes, which, of course, meant even more costumes and fittings.

How did you approach making costumes for the biblical period that was the setting for
Year One?

Jonah Hill (second from left) and Michael Cera (right) in *Superbad* (2007).
Photograph by Melissa Mosley.

Judd produced *Year One*, which was the last film directed by Harold Ramis. It's a wildly irreverent take on the Book of Genesis and was a unique creative challenge, since our ideas of what people looked like during the biblical period are mostly based on Renaissance paintings of biblical scenes. I took Harold on a deep dive through the wardrobe world I imagined for each of the characters. I had to dig far beneath the surface of what I read about the period until I could find something that I felt would work as a truthful visual representation.

I began researching the types of garments that might have existed during biblical times—exploring ancient textiles, pigments, and fibers to craft an authentic palette. In those days, women would spin wool or flax by hand or with simple tools, creating thread that would become the fabric of daily life.

In the opening scenes, I dressed Jack Black in the skins of skunks and Michael Cera in various animal pelts, but as the story progresses and towns spring up, there is more variation in the clothing. What a character wore depended on where the character was in the social structure. For example, purple dyes were prized and came to symbolize royalty, so purple became the foundation for Oliver Platt's opulent high priest robes, which were accented with gold, befitting his stature. The rest of the kingdom wore hues of yellow, brown, indigo, white, red, crimson, and scarlet—rich, earthy tones pulled from the natural world.

A friend of my son's owned a weaving company in Indiana. They loomed blankets for us using raw, organic materials, which became the building blocks of something ancient but alive. I sourced organic linens from mills down south, buying in bulk so I could experiment with dyeing and tinting. Every piece had to feel hand-hewn, lived-in, with its own history.

For the background world—nearly a thousand people—we treated it like a full-scale clothing production. I set up manufacturing in a Los Angeles factory, drawing on my years of experience running a factory for my jewelry and clothing lines. We went into full-speed production: tunics, robes, dresses, pants, tops—700 to 1,000 pieces of each. These were then shipped to New Mexico, where the film was set to shoot, along with costumes for nearly 150 speaking actors. I flew in ager-dyers from New York and

Bill Hader in *Year One* (2009).

Photograph by
Suzanne Hanover.

set them up in New Mexico. They created soft, dusty, beautifully aged hues, echoing desert light and worn stone. We handcrafted leather tunics and soldier headgear, assembled principal wardrobes and specialty costumes, and crafted accessories right there in our facility. We even made shoes, bags, horse gear, and head wraps. While we could rent some items from costume houses, many had to be created in-house to capture the specific world we were building.

Creating the Shaman costume for Bill Hader was the biggest challenge. He was covered head to toe with leaves, feathers, fur, bones, shells, animal and bird carcasses, a headdress with bones and bones through his nose. His entire face was covered in an intricate design. It was an art piece resembling the Soundsuits of Chicago artist Nick Cave.

Fitting photo of Jack Black for *Year One* (2009).

Designs for *Year One* (2009).

Illustration by
Chris Applehans.

The set, designed by Jeff Sage, was huge—maybe the size of a football field. It was shaped like an enormous fortress with stone walls, stone cobbled roads, and big, heavy wooden gates. Inside the walls were open-air markets displaying fruits, vegetables, and animal carcasses as well as stores and dwellings. Sheep, goats, horses, mules, pigs, horses, and donkeys roamed the set. And all of this was built on sand, and when the winds started and as the rain poured down on the first shooting day, the location became a logistical nightmare. Our team shared a massive tent which held nearly a thousand people, including hair and makeup and all the extras.

The Sonic the Hedgehog *films must have been an unusual costuming job.*

They were big studio films based on the popular SEGA video game and required some comic book-style, fantastical superhero type costumes. We were shooting in Vancouver, where my department had an enormous workspace, large enough for a full workroom and a dedicated aging/dyeing room. Our brilliant cutter-fitter, Gloria Chan, was able to create all our costumes directly from my drawings. The superhero fabrics were developed in Los Angeles. I had worked with these fabric people before, but this was the first time I was creating on such a large scale with multiple, complex costumes so I had to make several trips back and forth between Vancouver and LA to collaborate with the team there. Having Gloria by my side allowed for real-time adjustments every step of the way. It took several tries and some restructuring before we got things exactly right.

On *Sonic 2* we had more constraints created by the COVID pandemic. Since we were shooting in Canada, any time I came to Vancouver I had to spend 14 days in quarantine. It means that when there were problems with the construction of the new outfit I had designed for Jim Carrey's lead character Robotik, I couldn't be there with hands on to make sure the costume looked exactly the way I had designed it. Trying to fix a serious problem like this when all you could do was Zoom was almost impossible. It was only when I could bring in Joe, my longtime supervisor, to help deal with things in person, that I could finally put things back on track.

How did you start working with David Mamet?

I first met David through our synagogue. We knew each other socially, and I knew his family, but we had never actually worked together. At the time, I was doing costumes for a TV pilot—one of those promising shows that, unfortunately, never got picked up. David's wife, Rebecca Pidgeon, was cast as a lawyer in it, and I designed her wardrobe. We had such a wonderful time collaborating—she was elegant, sharp, and had that dry wit that makes fittings a joy. When the show wrapped, she apparently went home and said to David, "How come you haven't hired Debra to do your costumes?"

Not long after that, David reached out and asked if I'd be interested in working on a play he was directing, *Boston Marriage.* It was set at the turn of the 20th century and centered on two women in what was then called a "Boston Marriage"—a kind of deeply intimate relationship between women that might also have been physical. It was an extraordinary project: witty, cerebral, and emotionally charged.

During rehearsals, David would sit in the audience and laugh—really laugh—throughout the run-throughs. At first, I didn't quite understand what was so funny. The dialogue is written in this intricate, almost archaic English, full of double meanings and razor-sharp turns of phrase. But after sitting through weeks of rehearsals, one day it all suddenly clicked. I began to hear the rhythm, the musicality, the humor—and I found myself laughing, too.

David has an extraordinary design sensibility. At one point he even had his own clothing line, and his taste is impeccable: refined, architectural, and always original. We often went antiquing together, wandering through dusty fairs and stalls looking for props, fabrics, or anything that might inspire us for the show—or just for the sheer pleasure of discovery. He has an incredible eye. Working with him, I realized that he approaches dialogue the same way I approach fabric: with precision, curiosity, and deep appreciation for texture and detail. Working with David was a gift. He's a true artist in every sense—someone whose intellect, humor, and design instincts constantly elevate everyone around him.

How did you approach design for Boston Marriage?

It was my first stage production and a period piece, and David gave me total creative freedom. When we first met, he said, "I want you to go crazy." I asked, "Go crazy like—crazy crazy?" And he said, "Yes, go crazy crazy!" I even asked if I could design the wigs and makeup, and he said, "Go for it."

There were only three people in the cast: Rebecca Pidgeon, Mary Steenburgen, and Alicia Silverstone—three completely different women, both physically and energetically, which gave me so much to play with. David had done *Boston Marriage* years earlier at Trinity Rep, and the costumes then were traditional—all black Victorian—so

The cast of *Boston Marriage* (2005)—Alicia Silverstone, Mary Steenburgen and Rebecca Pidgeon—in costume with writer/director David Mamet.

Rebecca Pidgeon
in *Boston Marriage*
(2005).

when this new production came along, I saw an opportunity to reinvent that visual
world. I wanted to show that these women were ahead of their time—witty, trans-
gressive, and self-possessed, and who would have broken every rule of the era if they
could. My costumes needed to reflect that.

Design of a costume worn by Rebecca Pidgeon in *Boston Marriage* (2005).

Illustration by Anna Wyckoff.

Rebecca Pidgeon's character had this wicked, twisted sense of Victorian elegance. With her striking red hair, I imagined her in a vivid kelly green ensemble and another in deep burgundy—colors that felt daring, provocative, and totally her. And her hat—it was enormous, so large she literally had to turn sideways to fit through a doorway. I loved the audacity of that image.

Mary Steenburgen, with her dark hair and regal bearing, embodied luxury and mystery. I dressed her in rich black-and-white lounge clothes crafted from a vintage sari in my collection, draped furs, and sharply tailored suits. She exuded power and sensual confidence.

Alicia Silverstone played the maid. Her look began as a traditional Victorian maid's uniform, but I couldn't resist twisting it. From the back, her ruffly derriere was exposed, held up by an oversized, masculine buckle—and when she bent over to clear a tray, the audience howled with laughter. Later, her "found outfit," an extravagant Indian ensemble, was something I had designed years earlier for my atelier—a piece that had been rejected by a guru client. It was too fabulous to waste, and I loved giving it a new narrative. Her worn coat, scarf, and suitcase were aged and frayed, each telling part of her story.

The wigs were another layer—intentionally oversized and slightly ridiculous. Everything was a heightened take on period realism, balancing authenticity and absurdity in true Mamet fashion. I was delighted to be able to design this look from head to toe.

Making these costumes was no small feat. They were intricate, unconventional, and built entirely from scratch. I stayed with the cutter night after night, guiding her through the draping and construction. I remember sitting on the floor with pins in my mouth, bleary-eyed but determined. Every detail mattered. It was a massive stretch—both creatively and technically—but one of the most rewarding experiences of my career.

I later worked with David on his film about the relationship between legendary record producer Phil Spector and his defense attorney Linda Kenney Baden during Spector's trial for murder. I started fittings with Al Pacino in Los Angeles. Those were always an experience, but I had done two previous films with him so I was prepared. He detests fittings and can't sit still for long, so there was a lot of walking around and leaving the room. I had to be quick and meticulous. I knew that things needed to be comfortable, but since most of the clothes he would be wearing as Phil Spector were elegant lounging pajamas, it made things less complicated. The courtroom suits were custom made for him, and I lined both the jackets and pants in silk.

When I first designed for Al in *88 Minutes*, he had a few suits that needed dozens of multiples. I had heard rumors that he always insists on silk lining. When we first met, he assured me that he didn't need anything special, but when we had the final fitting on the suits, the day before they had to be shipped out of the country, he said, "Oh, by the way, do you think you could line the pants in silk?"

Did you research the clothing that the real Spector wore?

One of the most interesting discoveries in my research was finding forensic photos of the actual white blazer that Spector wore when he allegedly killed the actress Alana Clarkson. I zoomed in on the label and to my surprise, it said, "Laundry by Shelly Segal." Laundry, as I well knew, only made women's clothes. He was very tiny and wore small sizes, but a women's blazer is a women's blazer and it buttons on the opposite side. The forensic photo was grainy but clear enough to reveal the truth. Phil Spector was wearing a women's blazer.

Can you talk about how you started working with Dolly Parton?

Helen Mirren and Al Pacino in *Phil Spector* (2011).
Photograph by Phillip Caruso.

Dolly was the star of *Heavens to Betsy*, a series I designed costumes for. Dressing her was a unique challenge since she was world famous and already strongly identified with a style which reflected her country music background and a uniquely Dolly-esque glamour. Dolly flew me to Nashville so I could see for myself the wardrobe she already had and get a detailed picture of her style, its history, and how her style had evolved. In her house there were rows of shoes with six-inch heels neatly arranged on shelves. Even her sneakers had lifts in the bottoms. Her dresser drawers were filled with costume jewelry, sparkling souvenirs of a career that had always embraced glamour and excess. And in her backyard was a massive barn where everything that had ever been designed for Dolly, dating back to when she was a teenager, was care-fully stored and preserved. Gowns, costumes, performance outfits — decades of Dolly's career, all in one place. I spent hours there, combing through costumes made of cheap fabrics, expensive fabrics, intricate beading, elaborate adornments. Most of the silhou-ettes remained consistent, but the sizes shifted over the years. When I dressed her for a huge Dollywood Extravaganza — a show that took place in her amusement park in Tennessee, Dollywood — I used inspiration from everything I saw in that backyard but pushed the envelope to make poodle-style skirts with music themes, dice, and lyrics, as well as jumpsuits, dresses, blouses, and jackets. A luncheon for Calvin Klein inspired me to design suits for her using men's suiting fabrics, something she had never worn before. They were masculine fabrics but I used them to make skintight skirts and low cut jackets with a tiny ruffle detail in a contrasting stripe and surprise ruffles on the backside. And then, with only three days' notice, I learned that Dolly would need something fabulous for her 50th birthday party. This was a special job because Dolly herself was covered with tattoos and all her gowns had been designed to conceal the tattoos. But she felt it was finally time to show those tattoos to the world. I chose a gorgeous French gold lace with loops in the design, carefully placing those openings along the upper arm where the soft pastel ink of her tattoos peeked ever so subtly through the holes in the fabric. The rest of the dress was lined in nude silk—elegant and seamless.

Design of suit for Dolly Parton using men's fabric, worn to a luncheon honoring Calvin Klein, 1995.

Illustration by Otis College intern.

Can you tell me about your work with Tim Kring?

From 2001 to 2007, I worked on *Crossing Jordan*, a network crime drama about a medical examiner created by Tim Kring and starring Jill Hennessy. It was an intelligent, character-driven series—smart writing, emotional depth, and a terrific cast. I loved that it balanced procedural storytelling with real human complexity. While I was still on that show, Tim created another series that would become a cultural phenomenon: *Heroes* (2005). He asked me to come aboard to design the pilot. The premise fascinated me: ordinary people discovering extraordinary abilities and the ripple effect that had on their lives and the world around them. It was one of those rare opportunities where design meets philosophy—the clothes became extensions of identity, transformation, and power.

The scale of *Heroes* was unlike anything I'd ever done. One episode might move from India to Japan to South America to medieval Japan—all within an hour of TV. My core team was just twelve people, but on any given day we would expand to thirty or more, pulling vintage pieces, creating intricate Japanese armor, and fabricating costumes that needed to exist in multiple realities. We were constantly building, aging, dyeing, and producing multiples for stunts—twelve, sometimes two dozen copies of a single look.

I also worked with Tim on the series *Dig*, a 10-episode international thriller that he created with Gideon Raff, starring Jason Isaacs and Anne Heche. This was a different kind of adventure. It was shot all over the world, from the bitter cold of Canada to the ancient streets of Jerusalem. We filmed in the Arab Quarter, and one of the most unforgettable experiences was shooting in tunnels beneath the Old City that were still being excavated by archaeologists—spaces not open to the public. The sense of history was tangible; you could feel the layers of civilization pressing in around you. Working with Tim again on *Dig* felt like coming full circle. He has this incredible way of fusing mythology, mystery, and humanity—and as a designer, that gives you so much to work with. Every project with him was like a journey through time, culture, and imagination.

You've worked repeatedly with John Francis Daley and Jonathan Goldstein.

In 2015 they decided to take on *National Lampoon's Vacation*, which was a challenge given that the classic first National Lampoon film was directed by Harold Ramis in 1983. John and Jonathan wrote a funny action-packed script with two stars, Ed Helms and Christina Applegate, plus a fine supporting cast. When they asked me to do the costumes, one thing jumped out at me: on this vacation the Griswold family ended up in the middle of a Burning Man type festival surrounded by hundreds of exotic and eccentric characters, dressed in insane costumes. We had women whose bodies were

Medieval Japanese costume for *Heroes* (2006).

painted entirely in magical designs. Hair/makeup collaborated with us to complete
the vision. Rainbows, tutus, leather pieces, exotic headdresses—peace, light, and love
everywhere!

The guys hired Martin Starr and Samm Levine—my *Freaks and Geeks* boys,
now all grown up—to be in the scene. I designed elaborate costumes for each of them.
Martin wore overalls made entirely of blue, red, yellow, orange, and green teddy bears
arranged in a rainbow pattern over a matching tie-dye shirt. Samm wore a sleeveless
cutaway coat covered in seashells, crazy-colored capri pants, and an enormous top hat.

Then John and Jonathan asked me to design their film *Game Night,* about a
fun game night that turns dark when someone is kidnapped by dangerous gangsters.
There were plenty of action sequences, which meant wardrobe multiples, stunts, and
continuity considerations. Since the story revolves around several couples, I organized
it so that each pair had their own distinct palette, then created an overall palette for
the scenes where they all come together. Rachel McAdams had a leather jacket with
a striped sweater underneath. We had made a dozen of them. It looked like a sweater
under a jacket, but the sweater sleeves were removed, as was the back of the sweater.
The sweater cuffs were sewn in at the wrists of the jacket to look as if the sweater was
underneath. We did this on maybe eight of the twelve multiples to ensure that she didn't
get too hot while filming.

In the fall of 2022, John and Jonathan called to say they had a new TV show called *Hysteria*, scheduled to start shooting early in 2023 in Atlanta, and they wanted me to design the costumes and Joe to supervise. Set in a Michigan high school in 1989, the story taps into the hysteria of the Satanic Panic era. Dethkrunch, a band whose members are all teenage outcasts, pretends to be Satanists in a misguided bid for popularity—and all hell breaks loose. Packed with stunts, blood, and paranormal mayhem, the film tips its hat to classic horror while forging its own chaotic path. We shopped for vintage clothing from the period across Georgia. I also pulled dozens of racks from my friend Chris at his legendary haunt, Circa Vintage Wear, in New Bedford, Massachusetts. Then we received a surprise gift: 200 wardrobe boxes of '60s clothing from a recently wrapped show. Our show was set in the late '80s but all of the vintage clothes were perfect for dressing the older characters.

I wanted to bring something fresh to the genre—something not seen before. One big challenge when you try to create something new on a TV show is the need to have your designs approved by the producers, the studio, and the network. The young creatives who give approval typically have a narrow band of references, often limited to what they have already seen in other films. I wanted to go beyond what had been done, so our female lead wore a turn-of-the-century-inspired look—more white than black—with a rock-and-roll edge and layers of jewelry. One of the male band members had a visual arc—from nerdy to cool—which was fun to design. I wanted these kids to have the coolest look. We worked closely with hair and makeup but were sometimes frustrated with this process when the director got involved. Gavin brought his own flair to the guys' looks, adding patchwork, embellishments, and embroidery to their costumes, as if the characters had done it all themselves. That raw, DIY sensibility became a defining feature of their costumes.

John and Jonathan came into town while we were shooting *Hysteria* and told me about their new film, *Mayday*. Set in the late '80s, during the final days of the Cold War, the story centers on a Navy pilot, played by Ryan Reynolds, who is on a covert mission deep inside Russia. After his plane crashes in a remote forest, he is discovered unconscious in the snow and pulled to safety by a rugged, ex-KGB mountain man—played by Kenneth Branagh. It's a buddy film at heart: high-concept and big-budget, shot with the intensity of a serious action thriller. Layered beneath all that is the sharp, subversive humor of Daley and Goldstein. Britt Cox helped me prep the wardrobe in LA and begin the lengthy process of building the spacesuits for Ryan to wear when he was piloting the plane. For their normal clothes, we had great success with brands like RRL, Todd Snyder and Buck Mason that have a classic look and could have existed in 1987, at least for the multiples in this stunt-heavy film.

In December 2023, I flew to London to fit both Ryan and Kenneth. The fitting with Ryan was challenging because he was quite ill. We would ordinarily have spent much more time with him, but we only did what was necessary and finished in record

Emjay Anthony and Chiara Aurelia in '80s costumes for *Hysteria* (2023).

time. Kenneth's fitting was the opposite. We met him downstairs at our hotel where we had secured a suite for the fitting. We went through each change and all of the options. He proceeded to act out each scene, with each change, falling to the floor or whatever the scene entailed. He was brilliant and funny and warm and charming. With the final drawings and reference photos complete, we were able to get approvals and move forward with the specific costumes. We needed between a dozen and two dozen of each costume piece, all of which had to be aged and dyed by our team in Montreal.

Another dedicated team was responsible for background and uniform research since in one giant scene we would be recreating the May Day parade in Moscow's Red Square, circa 1987, with thousands of extras, many in military uniform. We were also tasked with creating nine replicas of the flight suits worn on the SR-71 aircraft. We consulted with specialists and ex-pilots, and visited several aviation museums to make sure all the details were correct. I even tracked down the original manufacturer of the flight suits in Massachusetts, less than an hour from my Rhode Island home, but the terms of their government contracts forbid them from assisting us, so we fabricated the flight suits in Los Angeles—helmets and all—recreating every intricate detail, down to the metal connectors. We built A, B, and C versions of the suits. The A suits were fully functional and capable of pumping air. The B suits were visually identical but non-functional. The C suits, made with less expensive materials, were used in background scenes and never seen up close. This tiered approach made it possible to create these incredibly expensive flight suits within budget.

The military uniforms—about 1,200 of them—were built in Spain at Peris Costumes. We hired a military consultant in Budapest to guide us through the process, while my team in Montreal researched all the specifics of which uniforms and medals we would need. Two months before shooting, I sent Gavin to Budapest to oversee delivery and begin fittings. We would be dressing 2,000 background performers in '80s civilian clothing, as well as military uniforms. We hired forty crew members and brought on an additional fifteen people just for the shoot days. Our reference photos showed dignitaries and guests bundled in winter coats, hats, and scarves, which we had discussed in detail with the directors.

In recent years, you've been doing the costumes for Jennifer Aniston on The Morning Show.

Jennifer was about 24 when we first started working together on *Friends*—so young, kind, and charismatic. I remember early on she invited me to her house to help her clean out her closet because she wanted her wardrobe to feel more sophisticated. We sat together with her best friend, going piece by piece through her clothes—"Yes. No. Yes. No."—until the floor was covered. Then we went to Fred Siegal, in LA, and picked out new pieces together. It was so much fun, and the beginning of a relationship built on trust and affection. Over the next ten years, I watched Jennifer and the rest of that young cast grow up—learning about life, gaining confidence, and, of course, success. I still remember watching the lineup of cars parked outside Stage 24 at Warner Bros. slowly upgrade as the years went by. What's wonderful about Jennifer is how savvy she is about style. In an industry where even the biggest stars can miss the mark on red carpets, Jennifer never does. She has an innate understanding of how she wants to present herself.

Years after *Friends* ended, we reunited on the film *Wanderlust*, directed by David Wain. We hadn't seen each other in years, but it was an instant lovefest. This time, she was no longer the young woman I'd met when we did *Friends*; she was a grown woman, confident and self-possessed. Our working relationship deepened into something more layered: woman to woman, artist to artist.

On *The Morning Show*, I design for Jennifer, while Sophie De Rakoff—who has a long relationship with Reese Witherspoon—designs for Reese, and Beth Lancaster, who started as her assistant designer, co-designs the rest of the cast. It's a collaborative, respectful team.

Jennifer and I have developed our own very efficient system. At the start of each season, I do a major shop—clothing, shoes, handbags, jewelry—and bring everything to her home in Los Angeles. Her dresser, Annie, and I unbox everything, line up the shoes, display accessories, and then Jennifer and I go through it all together. What

Debra and Jennifer Aniston on the set of *Wanderlust* (2010).

we keep becomes the foundation of her season's wardrobe. As each episode's script arrives, we decide which looks best serve that story and schedule fittings every few episodes—always at her house. It's intimate, focused, and efficient.

When I first began the show, I was shocked at how expensive luxury fashion had become. But I'm diligent about managing budgets. I negotiate with designers and vendors for wholesale and cost-purchase discounts, which helps a lot.

Design for a costume worn by Jennifer Aniston in *The Morning Show* (season 2, 2020).

Illustration by Barbra Araujo.

I try to keep our operation lean. I'm not on set every day, but I'm always there when a new look is being established. Otherwise, I'm in the office coordinating with Sophie and Beth to make sure the color palettes and styles stay in harmony. Occasionally, Jennifer will have last-minute inspiration and we'll scramble to make it happen—communicating changes across departments. But overall, we've built a rhythm that works beautifully.

Idiocracy *is a very unusual film that has now gotten a big cult following.*

Mike Judge, the Emmy Award–winning creator of *Beavis and Butt-Head* and *King of the Hill*, hired me in 2004 to design the costumes. The film tells the story of Joe, played by Luke Wilson, and Rita, played by Maya Rudolph, two ordinary people from our time who are placed in hibernation and accidentally wake up five hundred years in the future—into a society that has devolved into a garish, consumerist, anti-intellectual world run by corporations and stupidity.

From my very first meetings with Mike, I understood that this wasn't going to be a typical "futuristic" film with sleek silver jumpsuits and minimalist design. This world was *wrong*. It was cluttered, over-branded, ridiculous, so the costumes had to be as conceptually inventive as they were absurd. The challenge was to create a visual language for the future that felt believable but satirical, and to do it on a modest budget.

I started by thinking about what happens when design loses taste and imagination, when logos multiply and fabrics cheapen. We began building garments from plastic and spandex blends, layering logos and fake brands. I designed uniforms that were simultaneously comical and disturbing—an exaggerated reflection of our own throwaway culture. Every piece was engineered to look like it was designed by someone with no design sense at all, which ironically required tremendous design control.

It was one of the biggest and strangest creative puzzles of my career. We had to dress hundreds of cast and background players in this dystopian world, and every single person had to look like they belonged to it. I relied heavily on my manufacturing background and long-standing vendor relationships to stretch every dollar, fabricating custom pieces in bulk and repurposing materials in ways I never had before.

At the time, the film didn't make a big splash—it was released quietly—but over the years it found its audience. Now it's become a full-blown cult classic, often referenced in conversations about politics, culture, and design gone wrong. I still hear from fans who cite the costumes as prophetic or eerily relevant. For me, it remains one of the most creatively daring projects I've ever done—a satire that has, in many ways, become a mirror.

Design for the costume worn by the President of the United States, five hundred years in the future, for *Idiocracy* (2004). Illustration by Jacqueline Wazir.

Design for *Idiocracy* (2004). Illustration by Jacqueline Wazir.

Tell me about your work on A Futile and Stupid Gesture.

The film tells the story of Doug Kenney, played by Will Forte, the brilliant and deeply conflicted comedy writer who went from writing for *Harvard Lampoon* as a student to co-founding *National Lampoon*, a publication that changed American comedy forever. The story spans 1964 through to Doug's death in 1980, so it was essentially a period piece covering nearly two decades of social and cultural change.

This was an unusual project for me because it was based on real people—some of whom I knew. That made it both personal and challenging. There's a responsibility that comes with representing real individuals and a real moment in American pop culture history.

To create the costumes, I immersed myself in research—old photographs, fashion magazines, and fabric swatches from the period. But I also relied heavily on my own memories of those years. I remember the tactile feeling of the fabrics, the textures of corduroy and denim, the way shirts were cut, the colors that defined the late '60s and '70s—mustard, rust, avocado, and those slightly faded plaids. I also remembered exactly the kind of clothes people wore in real life.

I created each character, layering their looks with authenticity and specificity. I wanted each person to have a distinct visual vocabulary—through color, silhouette, and texture—that spoke to who they were and how they evolved over time. The writers, for example, had a certain East Coast intellectual style: thrift-store tweeds, soft flannel shirts, and worn-in jeans. The Los Angeles scenes had an entirely different energy—brighter, looser, more flamboyant. It was a film that required sensitivity and precision. It wasn't about exaggeration or fashion; it was about truth and tone—capturing the world of people who changed comedy by the way they dressed, talked, and thought.

Tell me about your work on New Girl.

I worked on *New Girl* from 2011 through 2017. The series centered around Jess, a quirky, endlessly optimistic teacher played by Zooey Deschanel in her first TV role after years of working in film. The premise was simple: Jess moves into an apartment with three single guys, and together they form this funny, messy, lovable chosen family.

When I started thinking about how Jess should look, I imagined the kind of teacher every kid has dreamed of, the kind who brings joy, color, and curiosity into the classroom. I thought about the books I used to read to my own kids, and those whimsical, eccentric educators who made learning magical—people like Miss Frizzle from *The Magic School Bus*. That was the seed.

Design for a costume worn by Zooey Deschanel in *The New Girl* (2011).

Illustration by Liuba Randolph.

Zooey had a beautiful, curvy, almost Rubenesque figure that looked amazing in '50s-inspired silhouettes—full skirts, fitted bodices, Peter Pan collars. Her style needed to reflect her warmth and offbeat personality but also feel grounded, so I started building her wardrobe around the idea of nostalgia. I wanted her clothes to feel like a love letter to childhood—a blend of optimism and innocence with a slightly vintage twist.

The color palette came to me in an instant: a box of Crayola crayons. I remembered that intoxicating scent of wax and paper from my own childhood, and I wanted Jess's world to feel like that—bright, playful, and full of possibility. Each outfit was a mix of patterns, textures, and cheerful colors, designed to lift the viewer's mood the moment she appeared on screen.

The show became a huge success, and I designed it for all seven seasons. What I loved most was that Jess's clothes evolved subtly over time—still fun and feminine, but growing more confident and sophisticated as her character did. For me, *New Girl* was an opportunity to create a visual language of joy through costume—an antidote to cynicism, wrapped in polka dots and primary colors.

What can you tell us about your work on Big Stone Gap?

I first met Adriana Trigiani back in 1994 on the set of Dolly Parton's pilot, *Heavens to Betsy*, where she was one of the writers. She had the idea to shoot a film in her hometown of Big Stone Gap, Virginia, and to include some of the real people who inspired the story in the cast so it would have an authentic sense of place. But despite securing names like Ashley Judd, Whoopi Goldberg, Jane Krakowski, Jenna Elfman and Patrick Wilson, it took nearly a decade to finance the film and production finally began in the fall of 2013. The story is set in the '70s, and I really enjoyed designing for that era's silhouettes, color palettes, and textures. But it was also an exercise in resourcefulness, in finding ways to do strong, thoughtful costume design on a tight budget. I was fortunate to have Nancy Gould, my *Friends* costume supervisor; my

Ashley Judd and Patrick Wilson in *Big Stone Gap* (2013). Photography by Antony Platt.

son, Gavin; the always supportive Palace Costume in Los Angeles, who provided most of the period costumes; and Jennifer Love Costumes in New York, who built costumes for Whoopi and Jane. When resources are limited, these long-standing relationships make all the difference. Unlike other films and series where I joined the project after it was fully financed and ready to begin production, I made a commitment to costume design *Big Stone Gap* without any guarantee of funding or a start date. It's important for a designer to take on projects like this and stay committed, even if it takes years before the film actually shoots.

Can you tell us about the two musicals that you costume designed?

In 2007, Adrian Pasdar—one of the cast members of *Heroes*—hired me to design *Atlanta*, a stage musical he had written. Performed at The Geffen Playhouse in Los Angeles, *Atlanta* told the Civil War story of a young Yankee soldier who assumes the identity of a Confederate soldier in a desperate attempt to survive behind enemy lines. There were eight characters to dress—soldiers, both Union and Confederate, as well as women, children, and ragamuffins. Nearly all the costumes needed to be bloodied and heavily aged, which meant designing and constructing them from scratch. With a limited budget, I had to run some pieces through my other workrooms—always a precarious task, but ultimately successful. Fortunately, I was able to call on help from some of the crews working on my other projects at the time, because the costume budget for a regional play—unlike a Broadway production—rarely covers what it takes to do things properly.

The second musical I designed was *I Only Have Eyes for You*, set in the '30s and based on the life of lyricist Al Dubin, whose songs include "Shuffle Off to Buffalo," "Lullaby of Broadway," and "We're in the Money." One of the writers, my friend Arlene Samer, asked me to design the costumes. This was something new for me. There were chorus lines, big dance numbers, and a large cast, all set in the glamorous world of the '30s. For the *42nd Street* number, I dressed the chorus line entirely in red—from their tuxedos to their dance shoes. The shoes themselves were a particular challenge. Dance shoes are essential tools; they must be soft, flexible, and supportive, and on Broadway there's often someone whose only job is to maintain them. I pulled vintage men's suits from costume houses, but every piece had to be altered for dance and comfort. We worked out of a ballet studio in Los Angeles that had a small workroom where we could quietly sneak pieces in for the seamstresses to sew. To make it all work on our tiny budget, I had to get creative—adding hidden stretch panels, opening seams, inserting ties, and improvising wherever possible. Then, midway through rehearsals, our lead actress announced she was pregnant, which meant I had to keep adjusting and even redesigning her costumes to accommodate her movement, comfort, and growing belly.

Designs of period costumes for the Geffen Theatre musical production Atlanta (2007). Illustration by Chris Applehans.

It was a real challenge to achieve the level of design I wanted on such a tight budget. Not for the first time, I turned to my own wardrobe and personal archive, searching for anything that could pass for '30s style. I was amazed by how many of my own pieces fit the period—a floor-length leopard coat, a green wool coat with a fur collar, a yellow wool coat, and several vintage-style dresses and scarves. One of the secrets of successful costume design on a budget: always have a great closet to raid.

Your work with Jennifer Aniston on The Morning Show *led to your work with her on* Murder Mystery 2.

Just after season 2 of *The Morning Show* wrapped, Jennifer asked me to design *Murder Mystery 2*, a large Netflix production that was shot in Hawaii and Paris. The story centers around two married private detectives, Jennifer Aniston and Adam Sandler, trying to rescue a friend kidnapped during his own elaborate Indian wedding. Principal photography began in January 2022, though we started prep early in 2021. Covid was still active, and people around us were constantly getting sick. We were tested daily and worked under extremely difficult circumstances.

The Indian wedding was the centerpiece of the film and my main design focus. I've always been drawn to Indian culture—the food, the colors, the fabrics, the beading, the jewelry. My first stop was Pioneer Boulevard in Artesia, LA's Little India, a place I've shopped for decades for both costume work and my own clothing line. The fabric for Phoebe's wedding coat on *Friends* came from a contact I made there, as did many textiles that I developed for my store. I used to create paintings that my Artesia vendors would send to India and magically transform into printed fabrics.

The vendor I worked with on *Friends* had retired, so my team and I visited every shop on the street, meeting owners and trying to find the right partner for a project of this scale. We needed three or four hundred costumes for background performers, plus multiples for the principals. Eventually I met Sakshi, owner of Dream Collection, whose company had everything I needed—beautiful beading and draping techniques, a factory in Mumbai, and the highest level of craftsmanship. She understood immediately what I was after. My team and I met with her weekly, bringing lists and sketches, and once the cast and measurements were confirmed, we began matching thread colors, silhouettes, and beading patterns. The early lead time was invaluable since shipping from India could take up to two months. I knew how unpredictable the process could be.

We made all of Adam's Indian looks with Sakshi, but for Jennifer's wedding gown, I reached out to Indian designers I admired. Manish Malhotra was my top choice. I selected four of his designs and requested samples, but because of timing concerns, I also designed several gowns myself as a backup. The Malhotra samples arrived just as my four custom dresses were finished, so we did a fitting with all eight. His gowns were exquisite and traditional; mine were more modern and hybrid in spirit. I suspected Jennifer would prefer mine, and she did—but I encouraged her to consider the traditional styles, which were more authentic to the scene. She was torn, but ultimately we chose a Malhotra gown and ordered four multiples, while preparing backups of my design, just in case. As the shoot approached, the Malhotra dresses still hadn't arrived, but miraculously they showed up on the very day of the fitting. I persuaded Jennifer to wear the traditional gown, and when she and Adam appeared together on set for the wedding sequence, I knew we'd made the right decision.

We shot the wedding exteriors in Hawaii and the interiors in Paris. Under normal circumstances, Hawaii would have been a dream location, but strict Covid restrictions meant no restaurants, no socializing—just work. By the time we arrived in Paris, restrictions had eased somewhat, though we were still tested constantly. Our costume department there was large and divided into two sections. Our French supervisor managed the background fittings and alterations, while our French assistant costume designer took me shopping and introduced me to some wonderful local designers. It was a very different setup from what I'm used to on an American film, but everyone worked beautifully together. Once fittings began for the hundreds of background performers, our office buzzed with creative energy and collaboration.

It isn't typical for a costume designer to do more than one movie or one TV show at a time. Can you talk about how you got into doing multiple movies and shows and what was required to make that work?

Back when I was doing Movies of the Week, projects were coming fast and furious. While I was wrapping one film, I was already working on the preparation for the next one. While doing *Friends*, I developed a close relationship with Marta Kaufman, one of the creators. When that show became a hit, Marta and her partners Kevin Bright and David Crane started producing other shows—*Veronica's Closet* and *Jesse*—all shooting on the Warner Brothers lot. They asked me to design them too. I've always been good at multitasking. I'm good at delegating and finding talented people I trust, and I loved the challenge.

The key was hiring people I completely trusted—smart, creative collaborators who understood how I worked. I'm very particular about color palettes and tone, and I trained my team to think the same way. I created detailed charts showing each costume change and its color story. We posted them in dressing rooms and kept master charts on the wardrobe trucks so everyone could stay aligned. Later, we built visual boards for each day's scenes with costume photos mounted on Velcro so I could move pieces around and show directors different combinations. This was all before digital software—it was our analog version of SyncOnSet. These systems made it possible to run multiple productions simultaneously. The boards kept everyone coordinated and allowed me to communicate clearly with directors and producers even when I wasn't physically there. I also made sure every producer felt I was fully present for their show, even when I was driving from Warner Brothers to Paramount to Universal— sometimes across town through LA traffic.

The standard studio contracts for designers usually include a clause requiring exclusive commitment to a single production. Over the years, I've been able to negotiate exceptions to that rule—often with the strong support of the project's director or producer who knows my dedication to my work—allowing me to work on more than one project at a time. In the rare case a studio insisted on exclusivity, I passed on the project.

Final Thoughts
Personal observations after a long career in costume design

Is there some other genre that you haven't designed costumes for that you would like to do?

It's not so much a genre in film that I still long to explore—I've been lucky to work across everything from comedy and drama to fantasy and period pieces. But I have always wanted to design more for the stage, specifically opera or Broadway. I think about it often.

When I first began working in theater with David Mamet, it felt like learning a completely new language. The process, the timing, the physicality of the costumes, the way they hold up under lights and movement—it's an entirely different world from film and TV. I loved that challenge, and I know that working on an opera or Broadway production would take that to another level. The scale, the grandeur, the sense of spectacle, and the freedom to be a bit more daring and stylized—all of that is thrilling to me.

There's also something deeply human about live performance: the immediacy, the exchange between performer and audience, and how the costumes become part of that energy in real time. I imagine it would be both terrifying and exhilarating—which is exactly the kind of experience I've always chased in my career.

How have changes in technology altered the process of costume designing since you began your career?

Technology has made a tremendous impact. Early in my career, there was no internet, so research was done the old-fashioned way—by going to libraries, pulling books, and visiting museums. There were no video calls either, so every meeting, every fitting, had to be done in person. These days I can be working in Australia and do a remote fitting with an actor in New York City. Technology has completely transformed how we shop. Instead of spending hours on the phone calling stores across the country looking for a specific item, we can now find it and order multiples online with just a few clicks. The same goes for fabrics. Whether they're from a supplier in Italy or a shop in downtown LA, it's all at our fingertips.

Technology has also changed how we prepare our materials. Our illustrators now create renderings digitally, and our mood boards, presentations, and budgets are all assembled using specialized software. Looking ahead, AI will no doubt bring even more change. As always, technology is a tool—an extension of our imagination—and while it may alter how we work, true costume design will always reflect the artistry and vision of the design team behind it.

Do environmental considerations play any part in costuming, for example, issues like sustainability?

In the last five years, our department, and film and TV productions in general, have made this a much more important and conscious part of what we do. Now we have procedures in place to recycle materials, and particularly recycle costumes which we have made multiples of. Increasingly, instead of taking costumes at wrap to a studio storage facility, we send some of them to outlets for resale or distribution to the needy. The fashion industry is responsible for a lot of waste and whatever we can do to reduce our environmental footprint is a good thing. All our dry cleaners are more earth-friendly now and use a greener process to clean the clothes. When a show breaks down at the end of a production, all the costumes that weren't on principal players go into costume houses so that future productions can make use of them. Instead of buying or building new garments, we use existing garments from our studio costume houses or rent them from outside costume houses.

Can you talk about the personal archive that you maintain—your design boards and drawings?

From the very beginning—going all the way back to the Movies of the Week—I have saved everything: scripts, research materials, fitting photos, all of it. When you're working on a film, those things feel vital; they're the center of your world. But the minute the project wraps, their importance seems to vanish. Suddenly, what was once so meaningful becomes just boxes of old material. At the same time, I have always felt strongly about keeping it all. These things become both a resource I can return to when designing future projects and a record of the body of work I've created over the years. My archive is privately held in our home in Rhode Island, although I hope one day to donate it to an institution interested in preserving costume design archives. Part of the reason I have held on to so much material is that I always imagined one day transforming it into art. About five or six years ago, I started doing exactly that. I began pulling things out of the archive—cutting, shredding, weaving, gluing—and then painting over the layered weavings to create a series of artworks I call "My Archeology." These pieces are, in a way, the story of my creative life. Each layer covers the one beneath it, just as each project of my career is built upon the previous one. It's a metaphor for time, memory, and reinvention—and it's an artistic process I can see myself continuing for the rest of my life, since I still have plenty of material left to explore.

What's your relationship to clothing and style in your personal life?

I've been conscious of style my entire life—it's part of my DNA. I never wanted to look like anyone else. I forged my own path from the very beginning. I wore a sari to my prom in 1970 because I loved Indian textiles and knew no one else would show up in one. Throughout high school, I always wanted to have my own look, and that came very naturally to me. When I was a young adult, I was a hippie living on top of a mountain, wearing wrap skirts I made myself. I remember cutting up denim jeans and using them to make skirts, thinking I had invented the denim collage skirt—only to later discover people all over the world were already wearing them. One of my best friends at the time had a pierced nose and wore beautiful, diaphanous dresses. The '70s was a time of freedom, experimentation, and self-expression, and from the start, I found joy in creating my own sense of style.

When I turned 50, my personal style evolved dramatically. During the years I had my clothing line, I designed with an explosion of color—my store clothing palette consisted of pinks, greens, turquoise and orange. I mostly wore my own designs. But I found that whenever I wore those colorful clothes in public, people would constantly comment on what I was wearing. I didn't want to talk about myself or my clothes. This is how my personal palette transitioned to black. And it worked. For the past twenty years, my palette has been almost exclusively black and white. Occasionally I'll add a touch of color, sometimes navy, but for the most part it's become my uniform, something that feels calm, centered, and aligned with where I am in my life right now.

And somewhere along the way, polka dots became part of my signature. I have a real affection for black-and-white polka dots. When I was a little girl, I had a black-and-white polka dot dress that I adored—it must have imprinted itself on my brain, because it keeps resurfacing in my life. Later, when I became a designer, I found myself revisiting all the dresses I had as a child. Every single one had meaning. I can still remember them in detail—the colors, the fabrics, the silhouettes. Many of my own designs were directly inspired by them. I once had a chiffon dress with a scalloped hem, and years later I designed a chiffon dress with that same scallop at the bottom.

Those early impressions stay with you. They form your visual memory, your design vocabulary. I've always believed that the things that attract us at 3 years old still resonate at 30 or 90. They become part of who we are. And that's what I tell people who are interested in design: trust your own instincts. Your inner design sense is already there. You just have to listen to it.

Shopping for costumes, 2017.

*What would be the most important advice you could give to young people who are
interested in becoming costume designers?*

It isn't easy to be optimistic about where the industry is headed. So many costume
designers and costumers have been out of work for a long time. Getting a job, especially a well-paying job, in any position on a production—and particularly at the entry
level—is hard, and every year seems to get harder. When young people ask me about
pursuing costume design, I make it clear that there are no guarantees that you will be
able to build a career and make a lifelong living in costume design. But if you are truly
passionate—if you can't imagine doing anything else—then you don't need me to tell
you that you must pursue it with everything you have. You may need another job,
a side hustle, something that can pay your bills, because there may be long stretches
when the work simply isn't there. But if you're persistent, if you seize upon every
opportunity that comes your way, if you know that instant success is very unlikely to
strike, your creative spark can help you find a way to make working with costumes a
part of your life despite all the industry uncertainty. Persevere, but also focus on developing your inner life. This is the most important advice I can offer.

Published in *Variety* magazine, a surprise gift to Debra
from *Friends* producers Bright, Kauffman, and Crane.

Acknowlegements

I am nothing without my crews. My heartfelt gratitude to the loyal and talented costumers, assistant costume designers, sketch artists, tailors, cutter-fitters and PAs whose dedication and artistry have helped me create magic:

Joe Mastrolia, Catherine Hahn, Gavin McGuire, Jennifer Iizuka Palmer, Roxanna Powell, Anthony Franco, Winifred Clements, Megan (Wiser) Moore, Diane Crooke, Nancy Gould, Julie Heath, Erica Arnold, Erinn Crane, Jennifer Grossman, Laura Guzik, Susan Michalek, Sybil Gray, Maria Grieco Turkel, Britt Cox, Brian Mahon, Roberta Haze, Dan North, Jodi Zimmelman, Sheryl Smyres, Corey Ching, Margaret (Rodgers) Powell, Kat Mastrolia, Isabela Braga, Lorraine Calvert, Mary Ianelli, Kathryn Gaskin, Anna Wyckoff, Angela Carper, Barbra Araujo, Andy Poon, Meriweather Nichols, Donna Chance, Paola Nieto, Annie Laoparadonchai, Lois de Armand, Helen Huang, Joseph Cigliano, Donna Casey Aira, Martine Gagnon, Henri Aubertin, Mathieu Hennion-Brossard, Sylvie Neant, Gabor Homonnay, Magdy Nakla, Esmilda, John Hales, Mr. Limm, Elizabeth Heszky, Jennie Baek and so many more.

The generous people/friends who got me started and those who supported me along the way:

Mark Canton, Stacey Snider, Gail Berman, Marta Kaufman, Mark Rosenberg, Jennifer Aniston, Adriana Trigiani, George Perkins, Nancy Josephson, Barry Kaplan, Melody and Lee at Palace Costume, Eddie Marks and Western Costume, Jim Livie and Eastern Costume, Katherine Pope, Judd Apatow, Jake Kasdan, Michelle Cole, Marlene Stewart, Aggie Rodgers, Julie Weiss, Sophie de Rakoff, Elizabeth Lancaster, Lou Elyrich, Bobbi Iona, Megan Needleman, Diann Newman, Shelly McCrory, Nancy Josephson, Nan Morales, Gina Medina, Sakshi at Dream Collection, Costume Designer's Guild 892, John Sacks, Claudia Sacks Schumer, Erin Searcy, Ellen Simon, Jacki Ochs, Ivy Ross, Gene London, Connie Tavel, Sabine Lelandais, Jody and Andy Snider, Kate Hines and Chris Hearn, Jessica Helfand, Seth and Cat Price, Daniel Heyman and Vincent Renou, Janine Lowy, Gail Mancuso, Wendy Shankin Cohen, Lincoln Cohen, Nita Tucker, Arlene Sarner, Bill Masters, David Israel, Mark Reisman, Chris Duvall, Jun Yamada, Shiva ShaMooil, Robert Lee Morris, Paula Silver, Harriet Stark, Billy's brothers and sisters and nieces and nephews, Rabbi and Meirav Finley, Chogyam Trungpa Rinpoche, Ida Bagus Anom, Alan Revere, Judith Linhares, Jerry & Joy Leisure, Babs Yohai, Chrisann Verges, Richard Nagler, Sheila Sosnow, Marcela Castillo & Family, Jim Carlin, Joe Di Battista, Ali Barone, Ali Heller, Claudia Weill, The Wiz, Jonathan Logan, Mark Hamilton Taylor, Jim Stark and Paul Cronin.